Bombproof Your Horse

Bombproof Your Horse

Teach Your Horse to Be Confident, Obedient, and Safe
No Matter What You Encounter

Sgt. Rick Pelicano

with Lauren Tjaden

Trafalgar Square Publishing
North Pomfret, Vermont

First published in 2004 by
Trafalgar Square Publishing
North Pomfret, Vermont 05053

Printed in Hong Kong

The author has made every effort to obtain releases from all persons appearing in the photographs used in this book and all photographers. In some cases, however, the persons and photographers identities and whereabouts were unknown. Should any names become available, they will be credited in future editions, assuming permission is granted.

Disclaimer of Liability
The authors and publisher shall have neither liability nor responsibility to any person or entity with respect to any loss or damage caused or alleged to be caused directly or indirectly by the information contained in this book. While the book is as accurate as the authors can make it, there may be errors, omissions, and inaccuracies.

Please note: *The opinions and training techniques covered in this book are solely those of Rick Pelicano and are in no way meant to represent those of the police force.*

Library of Congress Cataloging-in-Publication Data

Pelicano, Rick.
Bombproof your horse : teach your horse to be confident, obedient, and safe no matter what you encounter / Rick Pelicano with Lauren Tjaden.
p. cm.
ISBN 1-57076-260-0 (pbk.)
1. Horses—Training. I. Title.
SF287.P45 2004
636.1'0835—dc22

2003019071

Book design by Carrie Fradkin
Typeface: Giovanni, New Caledonia, Lucida Sans

Color separations by Tenon & Polert Colour Scanning Ltd., Hong Kong

10 9 8 7 6 5 4 3 2 1

This book is dedicated to my wonderful fiancée, Anne Boccia, without whom this book would never have been possible—let alone all of my clinics and the administrative duties that she knows I hate doing. She's kept me organized and inspired—and for her unselfish support, all I can say is, "Thank you."

TABLE OF CONTENTS

ACKNOWLEDGMENTS

Thanks to the great people at Trafalgar Square whose patience, time, and dedication are just exceptional: Caroline Robbins, the publisher, for her editorial insights and expertise, and Martha Cook, managing editor, for her organization and great help.

Janet Hitchen, of Middleburg, Virginia, took many of the photographs; she did an extraordinary job of making them not only helpful, but works of art in themselves. Foxcroft School, also in Middleburg, allowed us free rein in their gorgeous facility, and everybody took it in stride when balloons, umbrellas, and medicine balls bounced around the field. Thank you Sue Harrington and Nelly Sheehan for making this all possible.

I'm also grateful to Anne Boccia, Linda Emminizer, Mike McNally, and Dominic Pelicano who took additional photographs. Thanks to you all.

Thanks, too, to Gary Jones, whose great cartoons really enliven this book. Gary, a retired police officer, spent some time in the mounted unit, so he knows too well how horses can be. I've always known of his talent, and feel grateful that he agreed to work on this project.

I also want to acknowledge Laura Sheldon, my first instructor with the police department, who was responsible for recommending me for the training position. I have many great memories of us putting on training sessions and going to mounted police competitions together.

Thanks to my great models, who spent a long grueling day to get the photos right: Diane Wisda on Curly; Michelle Wellman on Carly; Lisa Monahan on Jasper Johns; and Mary Ellen Taggart on Baldwin. Thanks again to Megan Anderson on Remington who spent another afternoon with me taking yet more photographs. And, thanks to all of the great people from my clinics, whose names are too numerous to mention here, but without whom this book would never have been possible.

Finally, thanks to Jeff Kleinman, my agent at Graybill & English, who started this whole project. More than an agent, he's spent hours typing, organizing, planning, arranging the photo shoot, and providing great ideas that we've used in this book.

What is Bombproofing?

Why Bombproof Your Horse
Bombproofing simply refers to the process of training your horse—with a systematic plan—to become accustomed to many different circumstances, noises, and objects. This training plan will help turn him into a more pleasurable, submissive, confident, and therefore safer mount. In the United States, a horse that's truly unflappable is often referred to as being "bombproof" (stemming from the notion that you could set bombs off under his tail and he wouldn't react). Therefore, the clinics that I teach are called "bombproofing" clinics.

Obviously, this has nothing to do with bombs. My bombproofing program includes day-to-day strategies for managing your mount, as well as actual obstacle training where he'll be asked to tread on mattresses, push around giant balls, and march by flares.

Any horse that's been conditioned to be comfortable with a multitude of distractions and frightening circumstances will be easier to deal with, no matter what his job. Certainly, if you plan to ride in parades, bombproofing will benefit your horse because he'll be much more able to cope with strange sights and sounds. Likewise, anyone who competes in any discipline knows the advantage of riding a mount focused on his work instead of everything else.

But, even if your horse never has to set a hoof on pavement, bombproofing is still beneficial. Trail horses need to cross water, ditches, and negotiate all kinds of natural obstacles. Just convincing an uneducated horse to stroll by an everyday obstacle like a bush blowing in the wind, can be a challenge.

Horses That Benefit from Bombproofing

This book is meant for everyone. The techniques I will cover work whether your horse is a pampered show hunter, or a trail horse that's never seen the inside of an arena.

Imagine yourself in the following scenario.

You are hacking toward your friend's house, pre-occupied with removing bits of hay from your gloves, when your horse spots the tent a neighbor's child has set up. It's windy, and the roof of the tent billows as if a ghost were underneath it. Your mount jolts to a stop, and as quickly as a fly can land, he wheels and launches himself in the opposite direction.

As you struggle to haul him back under control, thoughts roll through your mind. *Stupid horse! He nearly ran us right into that tree. He has the brain of a hamster.* Shaking your head, you kick him in the ribs, and briefly consider giving away his carrots.

Whoever you are, no matter what your horse's discipline, this kind of behavior is no fun. Teaching your horse to submit to your wishes, and to be more confident and reliable, can only be a benefit.

Why I Know How to Bombproof

Let me introduce myself. I'm Sergeant Rick Pelicano of the Maryland National Park Police. I've been with the department for over twenty years, and, for most of that time, have been in charge of the training of horses and officers for mounted duties.

Although any horse that is accustomed to loud noises and strange sights makes a better partner, this is particularly true in the case of the police horse because of the nature of his job. He needs to be willing to stand for hours while children stroke him, but, he also needs to be willing to march through a

riot. Behaving in stressful situations is a mandatory job requirement.

However, many horses in the department are inexperienced or have problem behaviors that need to be resolved before they become suitable mounts for police work. To compound the problem, in many instances officers have no prior experience with equines. Consequently, over the years, I've learned the most efficient ways to teach riders the bare-boned skills necessary to make them effective in the saddle, and I've also learned the best way to bombproof a horse.

Right up front I should tell you that while I *do* use all of the methods I'm going to teach you, this book is *not* a reflection or a product of the Police Department or its policies. It reflects my opinions alone, and is not an official volume in any capacity.

My goal with this book is to relate the exercises and techniques that I have found most successful over the years in language that is easy to understand. From the beginning, I want everyone to feel comfortable. The one thing I *don't* want this book to have is "snob appeal." Don't be intimidated if you're not the most experienced rider—reading it won't be like reading Latin!

You might be familiar with the popular "natural trainers" methods. Some of them hint at a secret method of communicating with animals that borders on the mystical. In my opinion, the horse is presented with options and eventually figures out that the easiest option is to comply with the trainer. The round-pen methods that are in vogue offer the horse the option of continuing to move, or complying with the trainer and getting to rest. Nothing is wrong with these methods, but my technique focuses on a more comprehensive training program for both you and your horse.

Bombproofing your horse won't require you to purchase lots of special equipment, or invest in magical tools that I sell. All that's mandatory is the same tack you ordinarily use. I mention a few items in the chapter about training exercises that may make your life easier, and, of course, you'll want to remember to don your helmet and boots for safety's sake.

How to Use This Book

My method is a step-by-step training procedure that will teach you and your horse skills—from the basic "how-to-cross-a-stream" to advanced riding in traffic and parades. To do it effectively, however, it's necessary to read the opening chapters in sequence. Here's how things will work:

1. Evaluate your horse and yourself. In the first chapter, you take "the evaluation quiz." There, you assess yourself and your horse—everything from his breed and sex to the number of years you've spent in the saddle—to help you determine if you will eventually be able to establish yourselves as a successful team. It also helps you determine if you have the proper tools in place to begin your bombproofing mission. The quiz is simple and quick.

2. Physical skills. The first type of skills you need to bombproof are physical ones, and I address these in Chapter Two, *Basic Training Exercises*. I teach you to use your aids effectively and how to teach your horse to yield to them, and I introduce a number of specific riding exercises and movements. These will help you control him, particularly when the situation gets stressful. If your horse leaps away from a deer and scrambles toward the road and traffic, your ability to wrestle him back under control may well depend on the homework you've done.

3. Conceptual skills. Once you have your basic physical skills to communicate effectively with your horse, you then need to understand how your horse thinks, and how you can influence his thinking. If you understand your horse's motivation, it will be easier to comprehend why certain training methods are effective, while others are not. *All horses have the same basic instincts*, though they undeniably vary in intensity with each individual. In Chapter Three, *Bombproofing Concepts*, I explain how to both reward and punish your horse, as well as key concepts to bombproofing—such as the *comfort zone*—that you will use throughout your schooling.

4. Apply what you've learned. Once you have the techniques and the skills, you can start applying what you learned in the earlier chapters to really start teaching your horse to obey in difficult situations. In *Bombproofing Strategies*, some of my tactics are merely methods of avoiding problems or presenting lessons to your horse in a way that he may find easier to understand; others are exact strategies to cope with difficult situations.

5. Work your horse from the ground. One specific strategy is important enough to devote an entire chapter to it. It is groundwork, which means working your horse in hand instead of from the saddle. If your horse objects to an obstacle, it's sometimes easier to lead him over it first. In *Working Your Horse from the Ground*, I teach you how to do it safely and effectively.

6. How to deal with bad habits. I discuss corrections and preventive measures to use for the more common types of behavior problems in *Dealing with Bad Habits and Nasty Tricks*. If your horse has a nasty habit—like wheeling around or rearing—you'll find this section particularly useful. However, even if your horse is *usually* a gentleman, you'll want to read this. Even the kindest horse might react with some kind of undesirable behavior when he is upset enough. The process of bombproofing your horse can be stressful, so it helps to be prepared.

7. How to conduct your own bombproofing session. Although bombproofing is an ongoing process that is largely accomplished through daily training with real life obstacles, I do conduct special "bombproofing sessions" for police horses. I also give clinics for the general public that mimic these sessions. A typical session involves schooling multiple horses and riders over many different obstacles. The riders and their horses learn to cope with everything from bicycles to mattresses and giant balls. A session can serve to habituate your horse to many different obstacles in a short period and can dramatically increase both your horse's confidence and your own. A session can also be used to accustom your mount to a specific task, such as preparing him to carry a flag in a parade. In this chapter, *Bombproofing Day*, I explain exactly how I arrange my own clinics, so you can use them as a guideline.

8. Other basic bombproofing skills like riding in traffic, loading your horse, and other topics I haven't yet covered, including how to ride in formation and in parades, are contained in *Skills Your Horse Should Possess* and *Formation Riding and Parades*.

So let's get going! I hope you have lots of fun and great success using my techniques. It would be the best reward this book could bring.

CHAPTER 1

The Evaluation Quiz for Horse and Rider

Before you begin your bombproofing mission, you need to evaluate your horse's strengths and weaknesses as honestly as possible. You also need to evaluate yourself, which is perhaps more difficult. Taking careful stock of your horse and yourself—assessing everything from his breed and sex to the number of years you've spent in the saddle—will help you determine if your equine and you will eventually mesh well enough to establish yourselves as a successful team. It will also help you determine if you have the proper tools in place to begin bombproofing. The quiz I present in this chapter is a simple way to accomplish that assessment.

HOW TO TAKE THE QUIZ

Simply take the test beginning on page 14. But first, read where each question is fully explained to help you answer it properly. For some of the answers, you may need to saddle up.

The test will first assess the horse, and then you. I'll discuss the results at the end of the chapter.

Assess Your Horse
Disposition

The bold, confident, friendly equine is the one we all want to own—but if he's not that way now, you can *teach* him to be—right? I hate to say it, but *maybe not*. Schooling will always make an animal more pleasant to ride, and constructive experiences will definitely add to his confidence, but your horse's disposition and personality *won't* change a lot. He may become braver and easier to ride or handle, but *his personality will remain the same*.

This is something you may need to think about. Bombproofing is valuable, but not a miracle cure.

You can probably get your horse used to cars rattling by on the road, or teach him to stand in the cross-ties, but if he's a worried, teeth-grinding, generally flustered beast, that is likely how he will remain. Timid, shy, and nervous horses will continue to rely on the rider for confidence more than bolder animals might. What does this mean to you? If *you're* high-strung, nervous, or lacking confidence, you may be better off with one of those animals that is just this side of asleep!

A lazy or stubborn horse will need more motivation from the rider, but this type of animal is usually suitable for a greater range of people. A smart, quick-thinking horse can be harder to train, although very quick reactions may be an attribute in some disciplines, such as jumping and cutting. Some horses, though, think too much for their own good. When the "thinker" decides he doesn't want to do something, he may have several tricks to get his own way, like changing strategies and trying to capitalize on any weakness.

Horses possess an endless array of temperaments—but suffice to say, the more complex and difficult your horse's character is, the greater your skill level will need to be.

An "extremely tense" horse gets 0; "often unmanageable" is a 1; "accepting of new situations," a 2; and "unflappable" rates a 3.

Manners

When you groom and tack up your horse, does he stand quietly? How are his ground manners in general? Does he accept the bit willingly? Does he flinch when a hand is raised next to his face? Does he recoil when the bridle slides next to his ear? Is he head shy? Will he pick up all his feet? How about cross-tying? The general demeanor your horse exhibits can lend many clues as to the complexities—or lack of them—in his personality.

The beast that scores the best here possesses existing training, a quiet attitude, a general acceptance of whatever is being asked, and a mild curiosity. However, if your horse is an uneducated animal with bad manners, this doesn't mean he necessarily possesses a bad attitude. For example, let's say your horse is rude, stepping on you when being led and treating your toes with as much respect as if they were leaves on the ground. If your reaction is simply to shuffle further out of his path, this is an indication that *your* attitude may be the one that needs adjusting.

Of course, your horse is definitely not the head of the herd—that would be *you*—but countless people are uncomfortable with the politically incorrect concept of dominating another creature, even if the other creature happens to weigh in at over a thousand pounds and has no qualms whatsoever about kicking or trampling *them*.

If your horse is simply undisciplined or unschooled, his problems may be "fixable" in a reasonable time period. If your animal has never been punished for pawing—even when his hooves have come dangerously close to you—he may not know that pawing is an undesirable habit, and a few swats on the shoulder may be all he needs to mend his ways. On the other hand, he may be a nervous creature, tortured by the very idea of standing still, prone to fidgeting and fretting. Watching carefully and paying close attention to your horse's reactions will help you figure out if he's an aggressive bully, nervous, or if he's just used to getting his own way.

But it all counts. Let's go back to the above scenario, where your horse is trampling you while being led. Instead of merely tolerating his bad behavior, you get after him. An animal that reacts by moving away and treating you with a bit more respect certainly scores higher than one who reacts by pinning his ears in anger. An animal that violently spooks away when chastised similarly should score lower—because, besides bad behavior, he is also displaying a bad (or at least a volatile) attitude. However, the animal that politely keeps to his own side of the path and never tramples your toes to begin with scores the highest of all, even if the only reason he does so is because of prior schooling.

The horse that has a mind of his own scores 0; fairly minor bad habits gets 1; desires to please scores a 2; and amenable and obedient gets a 3.

Sex

Because we're talking in generalizations, I should add that our department only considers geldings for training, whether they are purchased or donated (I debated whether to add this paragraph at all, because I'm hesitant to prejudice folks against mares, when so many make terrific mounts). However, our policy is a fact. It's a matter of odds. If we start with an equal number of mares and geldings, more geldings will successfully finish the training. With their breeding parts and hormones intact, mares have a greater tendency to be herd-bound, moody, and difficult. Some police departments feel this is a needless bias and *do* consider mares; in fact, the winner of the obstacle course contest one year *was* a mare.

Geldings and spayed mares score a 3; mares rate a 2; and stallions get a 1.

History

Knowing your horse's history is helpful in understanding his behavior. Many times a horse's traits—both good and bad—are a direct result of his handling or riding. For example, if a person "bangs" the bit into his horse's gums over every jump, the horse quickly learns to protect his mouth, either by rushing, or refusing to jump at all.

Of course, sometimes an equine's past experiences with humans will add to his confidence instead. Many people "imprint" their foals—starting right after they are born—with positive experiences. This is the ultimate in bombproofing your horse, and I wish everyone did it.

You can make a more educated guess at the correct strategy for your horse if you know his past. A horse who refuses to get on a trailer because of an accident will need to be schooled differently than one that is balking because he prefers to spend the day in the pasture instead of at a show.

If you know he's been handled very poorly, give him a 0. "Had a mild traumatic event" scores a 1; "no evident bad habits" gets a 2; and if you know he's had compassionate owners in the past, who've neither spoiled nor abused him, give him a 3.

Training

When you ride, your aids—hands, legs (spurs and whip), and seat—convey to your equine the task you'd like him to perform. Like any other language, though, this is one that must be learned—not only by the rider, but also by the horse.

Do you think it's only natural for your horse to move away from the squeeze of your calf against his side, or drop his nose when you wiggle a finger? It's not necessarily true. For example, an uneducated horse often swings his haunches *into* leg pressure, instead of away from it. You might wonder why, but his instincts are easy to explain. The way your horse (and his ancestors before him) would deal with a predator clinging to his side—or simply an annoying bug—might be to edge up to a tree and squash it. To the unlearned beast, your leg is no different than that fly burrowing into his skin for a feast—it bothers him, and he would like it *gone*, by one means or another. The horse has to *learn* that your leg or your hand, or whatever aid you're using, is requesting a response instead of merely torturing him. Often, this simple logic is ignored. For your horse to do your bidding, *he must first understand your request*.

In order to answer the "training" section of the quiz, you may have to saddle up and go through each question. It is divided (and scored) in three parts: *Forward Movement*; *Sideways Movement*; and *Bit Acceptance*.

Forward Movement

First of all, does your horse move forward from the leg promptly and willingly? This is the most basic, necessary principle that your horse needs to understand and is the foundation for all of your other work.

Give him a squeeze with your calf. How does he respond? Does he move ahead? Maybe you need to add a tap of your heels to get him moving. This is not necessarily a bad thing. If you are an inexperienced rider, a super-sensitive horse tuned to listen to the slightest push of your legs may be difficult, if not impossible, for you to ride. You may *need* a horse with thicker skin, or at least a lazier temperament. Sometimes, it is beneficial to have a horse whose responses are duller and more sluggish and who won't react to the accidental slipping of your leg, or grabbing of your calf. If he responds reasonably, he scores a 3.

Does your horse proceed ahead when you ask, but act angry about it? An equine that merely shows some aggravation—perhaps pinning his ears, adding a swat of his tail—might be demonstrating his displeasure, but if he still moves ahead, he ultimately also demonstrates his obedience and knowledge. Give him a 2.

Or, does your mount react by doing more than only warning you? Does he act upon his irritation by adding a buck? Does he refuse to move, back up a step—or even worse, rear—telling you in clear terms that he has *no* intention of being your slave? If you get any of these reactions, your horse is confused or being disobedient—he gets a 0 either way. This type of reaction tells you he will need some schooling, or at least some discipline, because a horse that is hesitant to obey during normal circumstances will almost certainly rebel under stress.

Sideways Movement

If your equine understands what both legs mean (go forward), you can test his knowledge of what one leg means (go sideways). Go ahead and push into a walk. Without letting his walk get faster, try to scoot him over with your leg. Does he ignore you? What happens if you use your leg harder? Does he just speed up, pulling on the bit?

Try facing the animal toward a fence, where he can't go faster—in fact, where he can't go anywhere except sideways or backward—and ask him to move over again. Keep his head facing the fence, and tap with one heel. Does he shuffle over, or does he just splay his legs wider and look pathetic? I'm not asking for anything sophisticated here. However, if he *doesn't* understand, this will need to be remedied before you can progress.

Give your horse a 3 if he already understands how to move sideways from your leg, and a 2 if he needs prodding with whip or spur. He scores a 1 if he'll move, but is sluggish about it, and a 0 if it is a skill that he needs to learn.

Bit Acceptance

Another important part of your horse's education is his grasp of what the bit means. Simply put, when your fingers move on the reins, the horse should yield to your hands. In order to give the rider that wonderful feeling of holding hands with his mouth, the animal has to flex at the poll and relax his jaw. The trained horse understands that if he softens to the pressure of the bit, the rider's hands will soften back. This is, of course, *a learned response.*

When you ask your horse to slow his gait, does he pull his head in the air and push out his nose? Perhaps fling his neck forward like he's diving for choice bit of grass, dragging your bottom out of the saddle? Or, does he generously submit, reducing his pace? Obviously, this last response is the desirable one.

This isn't so difficult to feel. If your horse is gazing at a rock (or a rabbit, or a semi, or who-knows-what—he's a horse) and you ask him to look in the other direction, does he willingly comply, or does he brace against you? You can *feel* his response. When you tug on the uneducated (or disobedient) mount's mouth, it's as if you're tugging on a slab of concrete. The obedient horse flexes and bends like one of your own muscles.

The uneducated horse will tend to raise his neck—so that the muscles on the underside of it jut out—to protect his mouth whenever he feels the bit. He may travel that way all of the time (at least when he's under saddle) so he will be in the best position to evade control. His defensive, stiff stance freezes every muscle on his topline, from his poll to his tail. This stance affects each step he takes, making his trot jolting and difficult to sit.

An animal trained to yield to the bit can also be recognized by his profile. When the horse yields to the bit, his neck arches, his back relaxes (allowing you to sit much more deeply and more comfortably), and his hindquarters swing more freely. If the horse's face appears close to the vertical so his nose extends just forward of an imaginary line that runs

from his ears to the ground, and he's moving calmly in a consistent rhythm, then we could say that he's giving to the bit.

Educating your horse's mouth is an important part of your bombproofing toolbox. Submitting to the bit is a way of making him obedient and helping him to relax. Score him a 3 if he responds to light contact; a 2 if he is not steady on contact; a 1 if he has a sluggish reponse to it; and a 0 if he pulls against you, ignoring your commands.

Assess Yourself

I remember Clint Eastwood declaring "a man has to know his limitations." So should you! Taking stock of your abilities will help you *have fun and keep you out of trouble.* It's not always easy to look at yourself critically and honestly, so you might want an instructor to assist you.

Experience

It takes years to develop into a talented rider, and though some people learn more quickly than others, sheer mileage in the saddle *does* count. Do you have the ability to get along with an array of equine personalities? Are you talented enough to "explain," to even an uneducated mount, what you are asking for? Do you control your legs and hands well enough so that you don't offend the most sensitive beast? Any seasoning you have in this area will benefit you greatly. Learning on one animal that you trust and know is fine for starting out, but riding *different* horses can be a real wake-up call. What if you climbed on a strange horse and tried to ride the same way as on your familiar horse? Would you be able to get the same outcome?

If you've just started riding and have ridden only a handful of horses, mark down a score of 0; if you've been riding for fewer than two years, or have ridden only a very limited number of horses, put down a 1. If you have been consistently riding for at least ten years, and have ridden so many horses that you've lost count, you get a 3. If you're somewhere in the middle—an intermediate rider who has ridden many horses, perhaps—you earn a 2.

Strength and Fitness

Riding well takes agility, strength, and balance. It also takes a fair amount of sheer fitness. Your overall athleticism will certainly affect your ability. Give yourself a 0 score if your favorite sport is eating potato chips, and a 3 if you're fit and trim. You can rate yourself accordingly for all the fitness levels in between.

Experience Training Horses

By "training," I don't necessarily mean bringing along upper-level eventers or advancing your mount to the stage where he can win a ribbon at the National Horse Show (though it's *great* if you have that ability). The question is, have you ever taught new skills to a horse, like how to trail ride or pop over a box on the ground? *Any* training experience you've had adds to your skill level, because it assists you in understanding how horses react and think. It also helps you to judge the easiest ways to get the job accomplished.

If you've only ridden school horses, or your horses have always been more experienced than you, give yourself a 0. If you're training your horse as you are learning (and feel it necessary to have a trainer in order to teach both yourself and your horse), score yourself a 1. If you have furthered the training of several horses, or are comfortable training your horse without a trainer, you earn a 2. Professional trainers, and people who have started, and brought along multiple horses, get a 3.

Dedication and Patience

Horses thrive on repetition and continuity. A system reassures equines with its reliability. Dressage riders perfect movements through endless repetition.

While a *car* may perform the same way no matter how it was driven the last time, a *horse* is alive. Your mount has a memory, and he knows what has been proven safe and what has not been proven safe. Adapting a horse to frightening objects often takes patience, time, persistence, and repetition.

If you are impatient and just want to just get on and go and have your horse get over his problems *yesterday*, you'll have a much harder time schooling him (give yourself a 0 score). If you have patience and the temperament to work until he is confident—even if it takes longer than you think it should—give yourself a 3. If you're somewhere in between, score yourself accordingly.

Ability to Read Your Horse

Can you feel it coming, or are you caught off guard when your mount "blows up"? Okay, so you *know* he's going to spook when you hack past the same scary "post thing" that always makes him shy—but that's your experience talking. How about the time when he was suddenly five feet off the ground? Did you anticipate *that* one?

The best rider is the one who is attentive to his horse. How do *you* score? Can you recognize each muscle twitch? Do you watch him? Notice if his ears are riveted forward, his nostrils flared? Do you catch when he edges sideways, skin trembling, and feel what his body's doing?

The better you are in this category, the easier you'll find the bombproofing program. A certain amount of jumpiness is just "being a horse." This is because equines are "prey animals" and have instincts to prevent their being eaten by cougars and other "monsters."

If you're always surprised by your mount's behavior, give yourself a 0, and if you feel that you usually know what he's going to do before he does it, give yourself a 3.

Confidence

This is the big one! Do you ride comfortably or are you nervous? Do you love being around the animals, but when it comes to actually *riding*, you find excuses not to? The more confident you are, the easier your task will be because poise is something that you transmit to your horse. Your mount will tend to reflect your emotions. You're nervous, so is he. Some horses don't care, but they are rare creatures. Most *do*.

You need self-assurance to help your horse learn. The good news is, if you are lacking in this area, you can absolutely improve. Like your horse, you learn and gain security *from positive experiences.*

Get some lessons; find a friend to help you. Hack your "greenie" out with more experienced horses. Ride a seasoned horse and let someone else ride yours. But, do *something!* Riding can be fun and rewarding, an affair worth repeating again and again. Confidence produces enjoyment, which produces more confidence—a much healthier cycle.

However, you need to rate how you currently feel. If just thinking about saddling-up brings a lump to your throat and makes your guts twist, give yourself a 0. If you are only confident in limited situations—you only ride in the riding ring, for example, or only with others; or only wish to get on certain horses with a specific temperament—give yourself a 1. If you have some anxiety about schooling your horse, but only in challenging or new circumstances, give yourself a 2. If you are pretty sure you can handle most situations successfully, and think about riding your horse with eagerness and pleasure, give yourself a 3.

The quiz starts on the next page.

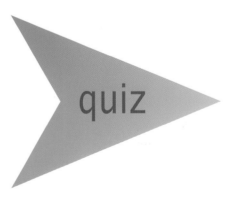

EVALUATION QUIZ

Rate your answers on a scale of 0 to 3.

Assess Your Horse

DISPOSITION   0   1   2   3

Your horse:

0 is extremely tense, nervous, and uncooperative to the point of actually being dangerous (rears or bucks for example).

1 accepts a few new situations after schooling; is often unmanageable; tends to become tense and act up when presented with different circumstances.

2 accepts many new situations without concern; possibly has a few known issues, but is generally manageable under most conditions.

3 is unflappable, willing to go through every unknown situation without blinking.

(For more information, refer back to page 7.)

MANNERS   0   1   2   3

Your horse:

0 has a mind of his own; is very difficult to lead and runs over the handler, kicks, and bites. People may describe him as dangerous to himself, to other horses, or to people.

1 has fairly minor bad habits that need to be constantly corrected: steps on the handler; is difficult to cross-tie and tack up; and resents picking up his feet, for example.

2 desires to please and responds well to correction, but continues to sometimes try evasive action to avoid performing in fairly common situations.

3 is very amenable and obedient under saddle and on the ground; stands quietly, leads well, is well-behaved for the farrier, and veterinarian.

(Refer to page 8.)

SEX   0   1   2   3

  1 stallion

  2 mare

  (3) gelding and spayed mare

   (Refer to page 9.)

HISTORY   0   1   2   3

  0 You suspect a very traumatic background involving physical abuse; he possesses an ingrained bad habit such as chronic rearing, or striking out.

  1 You suspect some traumatic or negative event in the horse's past, but it's nothing that would be cause him to be considered dangerous or unmanageable.

  2 There are no particularly bad habits evident; some exposure to a variety of different tasks.

  (3) Your horse has a history of positive events: imprinted as a foal; top competitor; has performed a variety of tasks.

   (Refer to page 9.)

TRAINING *(You may need to get on your horse to answer these questions.)*
Forward Movement   0   1   2   3

  How easily and eagerly does your horse move forward from your leg pressure?

  0 He is extremely resistant: either backs-up, rears, spins, really resists, or conversely bolts or moves forward uncontrollably.

  1 He is sluggish to the leg: requires frequent applications of leg, spur, and whip.

  2 Although not sluggish, he still must be ridden with some kind of extra prodding from spurs or whip.

  (3) He moves forward willingly with no need for spurs or whip.

   (Refer to page 10.)

Sideways Movement   0   1   2   3

How easily and eagerly does your horse move sideways from your leg pressure?

0   He is extremely resistant: refuses to move sideways when you ride him: even refuses when you push against him from the ground.

1   He is sluggish to the leg: will move sideways, but requires frequent applications of spur, whip, or rein; steps on himself; doesn't cross his legs.

2   Although not sluggish, he still must be ridden with some extra prodding from whip or spurs; will cross his legs over, and performs leg-yields, turns-on-the-forehand, for example.

3   He moves sideways willingly; no need for spurs or whip.

(Refer to page 10.)

Bit Acceptance   0   1   2   3

How does your horse accept the bit?

0   He constantly pulls, drags, and resists; unceasingly tosses his head; cannot tolerate the slightest rein pressure; grabs the bit; has an extremely insensitive mouth.

1   He has sluggish response to rein contact: will flex and bend, but only after a great deal of work.

2   Although not sluggish, he does not maintain steady, comfortable rein contact all of the time.

3   He flexes willingly; responds well to light rein contact.

(Refer to page 10.)

TALLY RESULTS FOR YOUR HORSE: □   □   □   □

Assess Yourself

EXPERIENCE   0   1   2   3

How long have you been riding, and how many different kinds of horses have you ridden?

0   You've just started riding: can walk, perhaps trot.

1   You're a beginner: have been riding less than two years; have ridden a very limited (fewer than five) number of horses.

2   You're an intermediate rider: returning to the saddle after a break of several years; ridden many different horses.

3   You've ridden consistently for at least 10 years; considered an experienced or professional-level rider; have lost count of how many horses you've ridden.

(For more information, refer back to page 11.)

STRENGTH AND FITNESS   0   1   2   3

How physically strong and fit are you?

You are:

0   highly sedentary: have an injury that may effect your riding ability.

1   sedentary: no debilitating injury; cannot get on a horse from the ground without assistance.

2   generally fit: can mount without assistance, but prefer to use a mounting block due to lack of strength and agility.

3   physically fit and active: no need for mounting block.

(Refer to page 12.)

EXPERIENCE TRAINING HORSES 0 1 2 3

What kind of experience do you have actually training a horse?

0 You have only ridden school horses or well-trained horses with more experience than you.

1 You are training your horse with the help of your trainer, as you yourself are progressing as a rider.

2 You are comfortable training your horse without the assistance of a trainer.

3 You have trained horses from unbroken foals to experienced competition horses or worked with a variety of horses with different problems or bad habits.

(Refer to page 12.)

DEDICATION AND PATIENCE 0 1 2 3

How patient are you?

You are:

0 very impatient: apt to use whip or spurs at the slightest provocation; dislike repetitive tasks; want to move on quickly to the next issue.

1 fairly patient: able to work through issues; look for the quick solution to problems.

2 patient: able to work through issues, but get frustrated after ten or fifteen minutes.

3 very patient and able to work through problems using repetitive tasks.

(Refer to page 12.)

ABILITY TO READ YOUR HORSE 0 1 2 3

How well can you predict your horse's behavior? This is a tough question, so there are only two answers to choose from.

0 You are constantly surprised by your horse's bad behavior, easily intimidated, and unable to formulate an effective response when the horse does something unexpected.

3 You possess a strong ability to predict your horse's behavior, and even in new or unusual situations, you have an idea of what your horse is going to do.

(Refer to page 12.)

CONFIDENCE   0   1   2   3

How confident are you when you get on your horse?

You are:

0   not at all confident riding your horse.

1   confident in limited situations—only in the riding ring, riding with others, or riding certain horses, for example.

2   confident, though perhaps some confidence issues—falling off in the past, for example—may limit your effectiveness.

3   very confident.

(Refer to page 13.)

TALLY RESULTS FOR YOURSELF: | | | 1 | 7 |

ADD RESULTS FOR YOUR HORSE: | | | 1 | 3 |

TOTAL SCORE: | | | 3 | 0 |

Results
Evaluating the Scores

If your horse has a score from 17 to 21, he is an exemplary bombproofing candidate. Besides having an even temperament, he has some pre-existing education and experience to help you. He should be easy to work with—if he's not already bombproof, he's well on his way, and the bombproofing sessions should be enjoyable for you and your well-prepared horse, and improve you both even more. No matter what your riding level, you will probably be able to work with this horse. If your own score is under 8, however, you should have some professional supervision.

If your horse scores from 11 to 16, he is more of an average fellow, both in his disposition and experience. While he may not be a suitable match for a total beginner (a person who scores under 3), if you have some skill and experience—that is, if your score is 4 or higher—you are probably up to the task of bombproofing him. The lower your score, however, the more you should consider having outside helpers—especially in the early stages of bombproofing.

The horse that scores from 5 to 10 falls on the more difficult side of average. It would be helpful if this horse is paired with a more experienced rider who isn't apt to get "dumped" when he spooks (which is probably quite often). He will need a rider with patience, skill, and lots of security in the saddle. To tackle bombproofing this horse, your score should be 12 or higher.

The horse that scores from 0 to 4 should be paired with a rider with professional-level skills—that is, one with a score of 15 or more.

What It Means if You and Your Horse Both Have Low Numbers

If the odds are stacked too heavily against you, you may not be able to forge a successful partnership with your mount. I consider a successful partnership one in which the rider is relatively safe (because safety is *always* only relative with horses). Further, in my mind, a successful partnership is one where the rider *enjoys dealing with her mount on a daily basis.*

One of the most important factors that determines whether or not you achieve a successful union *is the horse itself.* Time and time again, I see riders with horses that they have no business owning. I feel confident in saying that more people are "over-horsed" than own appropriate animals.

While we all like a big, "scopey" mover, an athletic jumper, or just have a soft spot for the equine with a long neck and a huge eye, the most important reason to stay paired with an animal is *because of your compatibility with him.* Repeat this three times and *never* forget it!

Try to accept your own limitations. Riding isn't the place to let your ego loose, or your emotions. If you're an inexperienced rider, *a more seasoned, quiet-natured horse is the best solution* in order for bombproof training to proceed. More experienced riders can bring green horses along *if* they have patience in addition to the skill that their years in the saddle have lent them.

Nothing can ruin riding for you like fear and injury. Nothing can ruin a young horse faster than a rider who responds to spooking, or a bid for control, inappropriately. If your mount is green and high-strung and you are also green and high strung, you are a terrible match. No advice, given in this book or anywhere else, no matter how valid, will be able to change that fact. One of you needs experience and confidence.

Never forget, you and your mount are a team. You compensate for each other's problems. What do I mean by this? Here's an example of how an experienced rider (one with a high score) might counter her horse's imperfections (one with a low score).

Let's say our rider knows blowing flags bother her "color-before-green-horse," but she needs to hack past three of them on her way down the road to the trail. The flags ripple overhead as if they are alive. She can feel her mount tense and raise his neck when they are still a hundred feet away, but she uses strategy to manage the problem.

Before her horse gets too wound up, she bends him away from the flags so he's forced to concentrate on what she's asking, and also so he'll be able to see an escape route. This, and her aggressive posture, helps to reassure him—just in case one of the flags *should* decide to climb down off its pole and chase him. In fact, her horse does try to bolt once, but she feels it coming and braces a hand against his neck, so he never really has a chance to build up speed. Almost immediately, he is back under control. The result is that they safely arrive at their destination.

Of course, in many instances, the horse is the one helping the rider, instead. An experienced, kind, horse (one with a high score) can compensate for his inexperienced rider's imperfections (one with a low score). Have you ever seen a beginner negotiate a course of fences? Busy clinging to the horse's neck, the rider manages to do little more than aim the horse toward the proper obstacle. Think of how the dependable old school horse balances himself, adding strides where necessary, taking care of business. Needless to say, if you own a horse like that, you are very lucky.

If your legs swing around and grip when you canter, you need a mount that is less sensitive. If you tend to jump poorly, you want a confident beast that knows his job and tolerates your mistakes. Sometimes, a person buys a horse on her trainer's advice, only to find that she's not able to ride the horse

without assistance from this trainer! You should always aim to improve, but you do need to be able to walk, trot, and canter your mount on your own without immediately facing control issues.

Low Numbers Don't Mean Problems Can't Be Fixed

A low score for your horse doesn't mean that you can't school him so that he becomes safer and more pleasurable to ride and handle. I'll discuss exercises to tune him to your leg and make him more obedient in Chapter Two. I'll also give you ways to thwart those nasty tricks he uses to get his own way.

A more experienced rider will have an easier time training his horse. A beginner will have to work harder, and longer, on both his technique and timing, and the payoff is certainly worth it. Nevertheless, a *beginner* on an *untrained* mount will be facing a difficult path. If your score is very low, and your horse's is as well, you may be facing an impossible task.

What If You Are Mismatched?

You knew it anyhow, but after taking the quiz, you can confirm that your horse is indeed difficult. He may be prone to hysteria when confronted with a squirrel, and may not be adverse to rearing or bucking, either. And, you're not sure you can whip him into shape. In fact, just keeping both feet wrapped around your mount's midsection is often a challenge. Riding him can get your heart racing as if you've just sprinted a mile.

It's beyond the scope of this book to tell you exactly how to solve your problem. In this sort of situation, you need to seriously consider replacing him with a more willing partner. Remember, this book is *only a guide*. It's impossible for any book to give you a method that predicts with total accuracy how successful you'll be in bombproofing your mount. Nor can any books predict if you and your horse have the capability of becoming a happy partnership.

Lilly

I would like to say this young Thoroughbred was a pleasure horse, but I don't know how pleasurable it *ever* was to ride her. Lilly was afraid of rocks, trees, even of leaves blowing across her path. Lilly didn't discriminate—she hated dogs and cows, and had been known to spook at other horses, as well. She was big "moose" of a horse and strong, quick, and agile, as well—she could jump sideways so fast a deer would be envious.

Though realistically she was too much horse for her owner, Janine loved Lilly. Janine also badly wanted to be able to hack Lilly out on the trail. Therefore, Lilly needed to go across streams—though, not surprisingly, she was afraid of water and refused.

I met Janine at her barn to help her with her problem. She borrowed another horse and I rode Lilly. I soon discovered that the available crossing was far from simple. When training a fearful horse over a stream, you really should have access to one with a flat, wide approach, free of hindrances and other obstacles. You need room to trot an approach and have margin for error.

However, *this* stream had a lousy approach: hidden behind a turn, it only came into view when it was alarmingly close. Instead of a smooth descent, the land ended in a steep bank.

Even if I could coerce Lilly to cross, the difficulties weren't past. She'd have to scramble up a hill on the other side, too. Both banks looked slippery, narrow, and uninviting. If Lilly backed up she could trip on them. Trees lined both sides of the trail. If Lilly resisted much, it would be easy to slam into them. However, Janine couldn't recall a better crossing in the area.

With some prodding, Lilly traversed the stream. She found the courage to go forward when she was allowed to follow the other horse. She didn't like it, though. She braced her front legs at the edge of the bank, slid toward the water, and then made an enormous leap *over* the stream. Having somehow managed to clear the water's considerable span, she then dashed up the bank on the opposite side, as quickly as possible.

We bounded over the water in this lunatic fashion several times. She wasn't gaining much confidence even with the repetition, because the crossings were unpleasant for both of us. Although she was being obedient enough to go forward, she wasn't getting her hooves wet, either.

I decided I had to figure out a way to make Lilly step into the water—and then *stay* there for a second—so she could learn that it wouldn't hurt her. Without knowing if she would perform the movement, I tried to position Lilly in *head away* (see p. 40) on our next approach. Luckily, she figured out what I was asking, and began to cross her legs and move sideways. But, at the last second, as we began our slide into the creek, she attempted to jump again.

However, her attempt to clear the water failed. Her legs being crossed, she landed right *in* the stream. She gasped, totally surprised. Her body felt as rigid as the bed of a pickup truck. But then, almost instantly, she relaxed, as she realized that she was okay. Suddenly, it was no big deal being in the water. We traversed the stream numerous times using *head away*. Then, she strolled across at a leisurely walk on a loose rein. Lilly even spent time standing in the stream, happily pawing water up around her belly.

Although by using proactive riding skills, I was able to habituate Lilly to the water, her unpredictable tendencies and frazzled demeanor made her a mount for only the most stouthearted, and this certainly didn't describe Janine. Though Janine loved Lilly, Lilly spent more time in the field than under tack. In the quiz, they would both have scored low numbers and consequently, were mismatched.

Many times a skilled horseman, through careful monitoring of feeding, turnout, and training, can manage a horse with a difficult temperament. Nevertheless, these strategies won't change an animal's basic personality. Ultimately, it doesn't matter if a trainer can cope with your mount. What matters is that *you*, his rider, are able to ride and enjoy him.

CHAPTER 2

Basic Training Exercises

Just the mention of *flatwork* is enough to make some folks squirm. With others, their eyes glaze over as quickly as a Minnesota pond in winter! But there's no need to feel uncomfortable, or even bored. The exercises here are simple, designed to help your horse become more obedient and user-friendly, and to help you use your aids more effectively.

Entire books—many of them—have been written about schooling your horse on the flat. These range from the classics written by dressage masters, to pamphlets passed out by local cowboys. Covering this subject in depth is far beyond the scope of this book, nevertheless, you and your horse will both need some fundamental skills in order to successfully train for bombproofing.

In this chapter, I'll discuss the bare-bones schooling techniques that I find most functional. (These are in addition to the basic walk-trot-canter skills that I

assume you and your mount already have.) Our department's police officers use these methods to assist them in managing and training their horses on a daily basis, and I think you'll find them helpful, too.

I'll also touch on skills you'll need to develop: a solid position—meaning an independent seat and hands—and a "feel" for your horse.

Every riding horse should understand the basics of yielding to your aids so you can control him, particularly when the situation gets stressful. Would you drive a car without a steering wheel? Or, one with brakes that only worked sometimes? Of course, not. However, that's exactly the situation you're putting yourself into when you swing your leg over an unschooled horse.

A racehorse is trained to perform a specific function—to run fast. Though racehorses require certain skills that are more complex than just galloping (such as the ability to obediently enter the starting gate), the point *is* that most of them can't execute a rein back. Most don't understand how to yield to your hand, much less move off your leg. That's because they *don't need these talents to be successful at their job.*

Pleasure horses *do* need to be manageable if they are to become safe, useful additions to your barn. In short, they need to be trained in rudimentary flatwork.

Basic training for you is just as necessary. If you are unstable in the saddle, besides risking a fall, your aids are going to be muddled and confusing to your horse. You also need the ability to "feel," because if you don't recognize the signals that your horse is becoming alarmed, your reactions will always be late or inappropriate.

Equipment You Need

As I promised in the beginning, you won't need any special equipment other than the tack you ordinarily employ. However, I'd like to mention some items that you might find useful, as well as remind you to wear your helmet and heeled boots.

About **riding helmets:** Make sure you wear one while mounted. Remember, you'll be asking your horse to perform stressful tasks. Even the best horse can be spooked, and even the best rider can be unseated. When purchasing a helmet, besides making sure of a good fit, also check that it's not considered "an item of apparel only"—look for one that's ASTM-SEI approved.

Heeled boots are another basic piece of safety equipment. This is because if your foot slides through the stirrup and you fall, you could be dragged.

Gloves are desirable while riding, and crucial when you're working your horse from the ground using a longe or lead line. They save your hands from rope burns and other injuries.

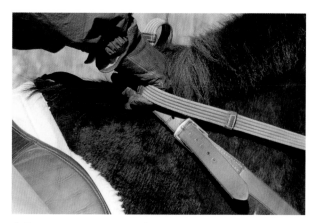

2.1
Neck Strap

Here, the rider has used an extra stirrup leather as a neck strap. This gives you extra "holding power," should the need arise.

Neck straps or **breastplates** can be used to give you added stability in the saddle. Riding a quick, strong horse, with lots of tricks in his bag is always challenging. A neck strap will greatly increase your ability to sit tall and deeply—instead of lurching into the fetal position—no matter what he does. But more security is *always* a benefit, even if you're only trying to survive a trail ride on an inexperienced horse or hack by a herd of sheep. It's much easier to stay on task, and keep your aids working, if you're confident that you are fastened into your tack and not going to get ejected any time soon. Using the strap is simple—just grab it. It's entirely possible to continue holding your reins in each hand, while simultaneously holding onto the strap with one of them.

You can either buy a strap made specifically for the purpose, or use the top of your breastplate. An even cheaper option is to employ an old stirrup leather, as in Photo 2.1.

Chaps give you a little extra grip, and therefore, security in the saddle. If you haven't tried them yet, you might want to. You may find you *really* like them. The only caveat that I would add is that they're *so* secure that when you ride without them, you may feel like you are sitting on a ski slope instead of a saddle. If you have a show planned where chaps are not considered appropriate attire, spend a few days getting comfortable in what you'll need to wear at that time.

Whips, crops, and spurs can all be used to lend a little extra incentive to the horse that's not sure he wants to go forward. All are only to be employed without anger, and, of course, a whip should never be used to beat your horse. While riding, I like to use a dressage whip as in Photo 2.2. A dressage whip is easier to use than other, shorter varieties of whips. This is because the extra length allows you to use it without first transferring the reins to one hand. All you need to do to employ it is to turn your wrist. That way, if my horse hesitates when asked to obey my leg, I can instantly tap him with the whip, *without* taking a hand off of my reins.

A short crop can be helpful, but to use it behind your leg where it's most effective, you'll first need to transfer your reins to one hand. If you need both hands on the reins, you can bump your horse on the shoulder with it, though it's not quite as influential there.

Spurs also reinforce your leg aids. The trick is to *not* use them accidentally. Inexperienced or unskilled riders often inadvertently bang the sides of their mount with them, causing a myriad of problems. However, they *are* useful when used appropriately.

Photos 2.3A and B show two types of English spurs—one is shorter than the other. The shorter one (A) should be adequate for our purposes,

2.2

Dressage Whip

A dressage whip is long enough to reach behind the leg to encourage the horse's forward movement and is used as a supplement to the leg aid.

although horses that require sharper aids and resist going forward, or sideways, or are generally dead to the leg, may require the longer ones. Photo 2.3C shows a standard pair of Western spurs.

How you employ your spurs is consistent with how you *always* school. Allow your horse the option to respond before increasing the severity of your aids. When you ask that your horse shift sideways, or

2.3 A—C
Spurs

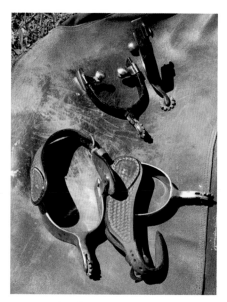

A. *A short English spur.*   B. *A long English spur.*   C. *Standard Western spurs.*

simply spring forward, the rule is that you first use a light aid—merely a request. A squeeze of the calf is sufficient, unless it's disregarded. *Then* is the time to turn your toe out and ask harder, but *not* initially.

If you can't control your leg well enough, you can substitute use of your whip, though it isn't as precise. In the meantime, of course, you should strive to improve your basics. Further, you probably *can* get away with using spurs in the walk, because your position is more likely to be stable in that gait.

I hesitate to even begin discussing **bits** and **bitting** because the subject is so controversial. All horses are individuals, people ride different disciplines with special requirements, and further, almost everyone has a strong opinion! However, for bending your horse laterally, a regular English-type snaffle—a bit that has a rein directly attached

to the corners of your horse's mouth—is more effective than a shank or curb bit. Further, a snaffle with a "D" ring works better than a loose ring for this purpose. (Some Western bits have a snaffle mouthpiece, but also have a shank that produces a curb effect. These are great for bending your horse from front to back, but they *aren't* so great for lateral control. Many times, the animal responds simply by folding his head toward his chest, instead of flexing to the side.)

Kimberwicks and Pelhams are useful bits for the animal that is somewhat duller in the mouth. Some of my peers only use a Pelham because they offer a lot of control. They feel this bit gives them extra security while under pressure, which it probably does, but it is easily abused when used by an unskilled rider.

The Three T's of Success: Training, Technique, and Timing

Here is some background before you get started:

Training is the process of improving the skills of either yourself or your horse, through systematic, graduated steps.

Technique is the way that these skills are performed.

Timing is the ability to apply the correct skills at the correct moments.

All three of these areas work in conjunction with one another. Like any other recipe, the one to produce a quiet, obedient horse requires all of the ingredients—in this case, the three T's—to be used in the proper measure and order.

Let's use a common scenario to demonstrate how the T's might work together to produce success.

We'll say you're hacking down a trail. You're enjoying the scenery, but your horse, being a "prey animal"—meaning one who might get eaten by other animals as opposed to one that eats them—is on the lookout for danger. As you round a corner, he spots something he deems worthy of his attention. A stump on the side of the path has been bleached to a slightly lighter shade than most of the other trees. He knows a real threat when he sees one, and he screeches to a halt!

However, your horse is not an uneducated three-year-old. He has been *trained.* He understands that he should respond to the squeeze of your calves by going forward. He also understands that you will reinforce that squeeze with progressively stronger aids, and that to ignore your request to keep going will be risking a kick from your heels, or even worse, a tap from your whip.

You have also honed your *timing.* Before your mount decides whether or not the stump is safe to pass, with your bottom firmly plastered to the saddle, you bury your leg in his barrel to keep him moving forward. This quick reaction leaves little doubt in his brain that you are sure of your intentions. Your solid *technique* keeps you balanced when your animal spooks one final time as he edges past the stump. Your heel is lower than your toe so your ankle can act as a shock absorber, and your hands are educated enough to avoid bumping your horse's mouth as you press him forward.

A lack in *any* of these areas—*training, timing,* or *technique*—could result in an unsuccessful outcome: your horse might refuse to go altogether, or at the very least, throw a fit before complying. Let's go back to that example again. Your horse has spotted the stump, and stops. This time, we'll say his *training* is inadequate. When you squeeze with your legs, he is uncertain what your signal means. Instead of leaping into action, he mulls the possibilities over: *Go forward? Back-up?*

However, even if he thinks that you *might* be urging him onward, he has no clue that ignoring your request is a bad idea. An untrained horse may view your aids as mere invitations instead of absolute commands. Instead of responding—almost instinctively—with an increase in speed, he questions the necessity to obey. And, since he isn't educated in the bridle or to your leg, bending him away from stump isn't even an option. If you *do* get aggressive and give him a good whack with your leg, his response may well be resentment: kicking out in anger, or even rearing. Obviously, you might be stuck at this bend in the trail for a long time.

Your *timing* is also critical. If you wait until your horse stops moving forward completely before pressing him, you may be sending the message that you're *also* unsure about the stump—or just asleep in the saddle, an easy mark. He might view your hesitation as a weakness, which suggests to him that escalating his disobedience may result in him getting his own way. Quick, accurate rebuttals to his resistance reinforce the idea that poor behavior equals uncomfortable consequences.

If your *technique* is poor, for instance, your hand involuntarily jerks every time you use your leg, it's confusing your horse. At the very least, your spastic movements suggest that he might be able to take advantage of you, and it's amazing how quickly his walnut-sized brain can absorb *this* tidbit, while figuring out that the stump is only a stump seems beyond him.

Imagine a chef trying to cook while wearing heavy gloves and fogged glasses. He might drop his spoon when he's trying to stir, and molding pastry would just be a joke. Without the ability to use his eyes and hands fully, his *effectiveness* would be lim-ited. The rider who exhibits poor technique has similar problems.

The language you use to communicate with your horse is mainly body language, that is, spoken with your hands, legs, and seat. If you lurch forward when your beast stops, your aids become ineffectual, and thus, your language.

Bad technique is also many times linked to bad balance, thus increasing your risk of falling. When you squeeze with your calf, if your heel is up and you are pinching with your knee, it's easy to tumble over your mount's shoulder.

Obviously, *all* these areas will need attention from you, as they're *all* critical. I'll go over the three T's in more detail, since these are the building blocks you'll use to help bombproof your horse.

A. Training

Training your horse is similar to training for any other endeavor in that you will need to work progressively and systematically to reach your goal. Just as an new, aspiring weight lifter wouldn't stroll into the gym and attempt to bench press three hundred pounds as a first-time lift, your horse can't be presented with a four-foot jump when his prior experience has been limited to skipping over cross-rails.

Training is like ascending a staircase. If you progress from one foot, one step, to another, arriving at the level you desire isn't at all impossible. However, if you try to leap from the first floor to the second in one giant step, it *will* be impossible.

This may seem to be common sense to you—and it *is*—but human nature sometimes causes people to cut corners, lose patience, or proceed to the next level too quickly. Of course, these "shortcuts" often cause failure, and worse, regression. If your horse learns to distrust your judgment, teaching him to trust it again is not an easy task.

Lessons must be presented in a way that the horse can successfully accomplish them and gain confidence. To ask your equine to broach what may appear to him to be insurmountable tasks can be very damaging, resulting in frustration, confusion, and anxiety on the part of *both* horse and human.

It's my own personal philosophy that horse and rider can both benefit from a well-rounded education, but many riders seem reluctant to stray from their specialty. Some dressage enthusiasts shudder at the thought of trotting a fence, while steeplechase lovers may scoff at the notion of a horse flexing at the poll.

Training in different disciplines will teach you different strengths, and those strengths add to your chance of building a successful partnership with your animal. If your discipline is hunters, spend some time working on dressage. No matter how good you are at "finding" those eight fences, it's still easier on a horse that can move laterally and understands what the bit means. Even if you love half-pass and could care less about hacking out, learning to ride aggressively and how to balance over the differing terrain can only be an asset.

Once the horse and rider are compatible, they can both strive to improve. Riders should always work on perfecting their basics. The building blocks of riding will never change. This is a martial arts concept that applies well to horsemanship. It's wonderful to train at an advanced level, but advanced concepts—whether we're talking about dressage, reining, or just obedience—*are always derived from basics.*

If your animal has basic training, lengthening or shortening his stride isn't so difficult. If he accepts the rider's hand and leg, bending him one way or another is simple. However, if your basics are incorrect, your advanced work will be as well. If your horse pulls the reins out of your hands, hollows his back, or sulks when the leg is applied, the simplest

movements may become impossibilities. A responsive, trained horse, schooled in a well-rounded manner, is certainly much easier to bombproof.

The correct foundation for your horse means that he possesses straightness, impulsion, rhythm, and submission. The rider needs to develop empathy and understanding for her horse, as well as a correct position and effective aids. The pair enjoying these strengths will undeniably have an advantage over the vast majority of their peers. You both need to become proficient in *at least* the following areas:

1 Your mount will need to be able to work at all three gaits in a consistent rhythm, traveling straight, moving with impulsion, remaining reasonably obedient. This schooling will make him more controllable and responsive.

2 Your mount should also understand basic lateral movements. Don't be unnerved if this term is unfamiliar. Lateral work simply means that he knows how to move sideways, as well as forward. He'll also need to learn to back-up and to stand still when asked. I'll specify the exact training exercises I like to use later in this chapter.

3 I also feel that all horses should learn how to hop over small obstacles. I'm not talking about anything complicated, just the ability to jump a small ditch or log, and be able to travel up or down a bank. This is a practical skill for trail riding but also useful psychologically.

4 Whether or not you have interest in carrying bombproofing to a higher level—teaching your mount to carry a flag or traipse through a riot—I feel all horses should be trained to be able to handle the common situations that they will encounter to be useful in everyday life. You should be able to ride your animal in traffic. No, not necessarily through New York City or the center of London, but you should be able to hack down a country lane, either in the company of another horse or by yourselves, and have a tractor pass without either of you having heart palpitations.

5 Your horse should stand quietly while being mounted.

6 Without fuss, he must load in the horse trailer or van and allow himself to be transported.

7 He ought to exhibit good stable manners when being clipped, shod, or groomed, and, of course, when being tacked-up.

After he's become skilled in all these areas, you can advance to more challenging situations, if you please, but these are the minimum abilities that the serviceable animal needs to have.

Whenever you train, you need to work your horse in a progressive manner. Determine your horse's *comfort zone* (see p. 49), and work within it, repeating the lesson until he is no longer alarmed by it. Make the lesson harder—increase its intensity— only when your horse has accepted the easier one. Let your horse decide when he's ready to progress. It's a decision you can't make for him. Try to be patient and listen to what he's telling you. Some horses require more time than others.

Active riding skills are those used specifically to get your horse through a challenging circumstance. Many of these skills have a basis in dressage. To use them successfully, you need to think ahead, know

your horse, and understand *his* thinking processes. These things will help you choose the best strategy available. Remember, the more training you and your horse have, the more options will be accessible. Correct execution of technique at the right time will give you optimum results.

B. Technique

If your *technique* is insufficient, your results will be, as well. No matter how determined you are, without a balanced, effective position you are doomed to failure. The reason for poor technique is usually inexperience or the lack of decent instruction. A lack of experience can simply be cured by more of it, and finding someone to help you with your riding is probably not impossible, either.

One thing that *is* difficult to teach, though, is the ability to read a horse's intentions, and to apply the appropriate technique to the circumstance. Since horses are as individual as people, dealing with them can never be as absolute as dealing with a machine. In a car, if you step on the brakes, the car responds by slowing down. If the brakes don't work, you'll take your car to a mechanic.

Riding is more complicated. Your horse's brakes might not be functioning for *all kinds* of reasons. Your horse may just be distracted, or may not be educated enough to understand your command. He might be ignoring your command because he's busy watching a horse in the next field. Because living creatures with their own agendas are involved, the rider needs to analyze every situation and attempt to figure out why, indeed, the brakes have failed, or why her animal isn't responding. Often, the rider is simply doing the wrong thing at the wrong time.

Many times in clinics, I've offered advice to students when their horses refuse to negotiate an obstacle. Often, the student will *swear* that she's using her aids correctly, yet, when I get on, the horse performs. Occasionally, I have misread the horse and, once mounted, find a different strategy is called for. However, *usually* the horse either has no confidence in his rider or is confused.

Often, the rider thinks she is doing the things I've suggested but fails to see that the correct amount of energy she needs to put into her aids is the amount that it takes the horse to respond. On a scale of one to ten (of how hard a rider needs to kick or pull, or just look where she wants to go), she may have needed to use at least at an eight to succeed, but she may have been stuck at only about a three.

Because training is a new experience to many riders, it is important to be critical and analytical of yourself and think about what you could have done to improve the situation, instead of only blaming the horse.

During one clinic, I had a student who attempted the mattress obstacle, but had difficulty in pushing her horse over it. The more I asked her to steer and gaze where she wanted to be heading, the more she clutched and sank into her horse's mane, causing her aids to become ineffective. Later, at the end of the clinic, we played soccer on the horses with the big ball. She and her horse crossed over that same mattress *repeatedly*. Her aids became effective when she was no longer worrying about the mattress, and she became distracted by her interest in the game.

A more seasoned rider will always have more chance of successfully schooling her animal with a particular problem, because slight variations in technique can have a huge cumulative effect. However, *none* of us can expect perfection—in our horses, or ourselves. But, you need to strive to achieve the best personal skills you can in order to reduce the frustration of your horse and yourself.

C. Timing

Timing is critical in many areas of life, and is absolutely necessary in order to have success with bombproofing your horse. An important aspect of timing is the ability to read your horse's intentions and to perceive problems ahead of time.

Have you have ever ridden a lazy horse that needs to have the aids applied over and over again? A skilled rider will make corrections before the horse slows or breaks his rhythm at all, and will create the perception of a willing, forward animal. However, the unskilled rider won't feel the horse hesitate until he has almost broken to the next, slower gait. Being unable to anticipate—or, at least react to what each of the horse's movements is suggesting—allows the horse's gaits to become inconsistent. The beast may well lurch into a walk and then scramble into a canter. This skill, the ability to do the right thing at the right time, is partly learned, partly instinctual. It isn't an easy one to teach.

Timing is just as critical when correcting or preventing misbehavior. If, when I'm riding down the trail, I feel my horse begin to hesitate and perhaps raise his head, I react immediately. I take preventive action. Perhaps I'll take his head away from the object and I'll increase his impulsion—push him forward—if not actually increasing the speed.

If I do nothing, my horse may refuse to move forward altogether. If I let my mount focus intently on the scary object, his fears may become amplified, particularly as I get closer to it. But, even if I've blundered by, waiting to react, once my horse does, I have to, too. My response *must* be immediate. A delayed reaction on my part will cause the problem to worsen.

The timing factor in this type of situation is critical because if I was riding actively in the beginning, I might have prevented or minimized his adverse reaction entirely.

George

I once went to two barns in separate locations, which were run under one management. Several stalls in Barn A were having their flooring replaced, and it was decided that one of the horses who lived there, an Appaloosa gelding named George, needed to take up temporary residence in Barn B so the work could be accomplished.

Although George wasn't tall, he was stout. He wasn't the most refined horse: a hammer-shaped profile, zebra-like mane, and thick neck which poked out of his shoulder like a shapeless hunk of meat.

In any case, it was necessary for George to be trailered to Barn B. Curly, so nicknamed because of her unruly hair, was in charge at Barn A. She was the first to try to load George onto the trailer. George decided he wasn't inclined to comply, and though he didn't rear or threaten to throw himself over backwards, he made his feelings known nevertheless. He first swerved to the side of the ramp; when straightened, he balked. Curly quickly decided George was afraid. She stroked his neck and murmured to him, but George remained unconvinced. So Curly elected to try a mystical training technique she read about in a holistic horse magazine. When this method failed, she resorted to the old "food bribe method," but was once again unsuccessful. While George would tiptoe up the ramp to slurp grain from her hand, he wasn't hungry enough to follow her further. Curly's subsequent ploy was to institute help from two other barn workers.

To no avail! Curly played with George's muzzle while she informed him that he was being bad. The barn help tried to push his bottom in line with the ramp, but whenever they clicked too much or waved their arms at him, Curly would warn them that he was only scared and that they shouldn't pressure him. The problem escalated. In an effort to thwart George from running to the side to avoid the trailer entrance, Curly finally backed the trailer to the door of the barn.

George didn't look much frightened to me—in fact, he was the only one who was content. He swatted his scanty tail in the helper's faces and stood on their feet while Curly tried to tempt him with more grain. Between the action, Curly rushed to make several frantic calls to the barn manager at Barn B, Melissa.

Curly sighed as she reported Melissa's advice to us. "She says there's nothing wrong with George. She says he's not afraid, to stop bribing him, stop the voodoo, and just load him like you mean it." She brushed a ringlet from her eyes. "I wish Melissa was here. Then she could see for herself how impossible he's being."

An hour later, Curly got her wish. Melissa decided that the only way George was going to load was if she did it herself. She told Curly to stop what she was doing and put the horse in a stall. When Melissa arrived, she marched straight to George's stall. Her jaw was clenched as she haltered him. She bumped him with the lead rope and growled at him as she led him from the stall.

"If you don't get on the trailer, I'll have you for dinner," she warned.

We all watched and waited. But Melissa just strode toward the trailer and growled one more time. George walked on. In fact, he followed as meekly as a plow horse.

The lesson here is that George's handlers hadn't the *technique* to accomplish their task. They formulated an inappropriate strategy based on an erroneous assessment of the situation. They tried to baby and bribe a horse that was not afraid. All George needed was confident, meaningful direction, and immediate correction (and this is where *timing* comes in, as well) of his unwanted, evasive behavior. And actually, Melissa didn't *have* to correct anything, since George immediately complied when confronted with someone who obviously meant business.

As we'll discuss in detail in a moment, you should always have empathy for your horse, you should always ask him only questions that are reasonable, and the punishment (*such* a politically incorrect word) you dole out should never be a result of temper. However, this doesn't mean that your horse will do your bidding simply because he loves you. That only works in children's movies. Hopefully, eventually you and your horse will form a strong partnership, where you both trust and have confidence in each other. Hopefully, your horse will learn to take pleasure in his work. But your horse, no matter how fond you are of him, must realize that his behavior always results in subsequent action—either positive or negative.

Now you understand my philosophy and have the basic understanding of what we're going to be talking about. I'm now going to discuss specific exercises to develop your basic skills and training.

Specific Exercises
Exercise 1: Going Forward

Riding a bike can be hard work. As soon as you stop pedaling, *it'll* stop, too—unless you're coasting downhill, of course. Your horse shouldn't require so much effort. He can, however, become desensitized to your driving aids, and end up responding to your leg in almost the same fashion as the bike. Of course, when you have to "pedal" your mount—squeezing and prodding just to keep him shuffling along at the same pace—it takes a lot of the enjoyment out of riding. Further, when you need him to react quickly (such as when you're cantering toward a fence you mean to jump, and he slows down), his delayed, sluggish response may come back to bite you. You need to make sure your horse responds to your requests to go forward, and in fairly short order.

The first thing that I want you to do, before you worry about teaching your horse any of the other exercises I list, is verify that your mount moves smartly forward when you ask.

Testing Your Horse's Response

So, does your horse respect your leg, or does he take his time before responding? You probably already know if the "procrastinating pony" we're talking about is *yours*, but if you're not sure, it's easy to test him. Mount up, and press your calf against him. If you can count to more than "one-thousand-one" before he moves, you have some homework to do. If your horse pushes off sharply, congratulations—you can skip this exercise.

If your horse is ignoring you, you need to work on your *own* reactions to strengthen your horse's response. Though some horses are certainly more sensitive than others, if your horse ignores you, the responsibility is ultimately yours. A horse that doesn't respect your leg has not been *made* to respect your leg. As always, when schooling your mount, his behavior needs to carry consequences.

The correct rebuttal when your horse disregards a command to go forward is to reinforce the originally applied aid with an increasingly stronger one. In other words, if your horse only snores when you apply leg pressure, you should—instantly—give him a sharp tap with your heels. If this request is similarly ignored, your next action should be to give him a stiffer kick, and perhaps add a reminder with a flick of your whip. Ideally, the whip should be used right behind your leg. This makes it clearer to your horse that the whip is associated with your leg aids. Further, since the whip is being used behind his center,

he'll tend to go forward to get away from it. You can substitute by tapping your horse on his shoulder instead, if you have good reason—a violent spook, for instance—and you're afraid you're going to fall off if you let go of the reins to give him a smack.

While the correct amount of aid is the amount needed to get the job done, you always want to ask your horse to obey with the minimal aid first. You shouldn't *assume* that your horse will ignore your request, and start by using your dressage whip. He should always have the chance to prove that he is indeed listening. Otherwise, you're punishing him for something that he hasn't yet done.

The other caveat that I would offer is the obvious one. Your whip is an aid, designed to add influence. It should never be used to beat your horse, or on his face, or in temper. If you're furious, you need to dismount and grab a deep breath, so you can effectively resume your role as your horse's teacher.

Your horse should get in the habit of expecting you to insist on his attention, just as you should get in the habit of insisting on it. When he responds to your leg, whether he is halted or already moving, by distinctly increasing his pace, your mount has absorbed this lesson. (Of course, this doesn't mean he won't soon forget to obey you, if given the chance.)

You have mastered this lesson when you don't need to think about it before doing it. When your heel gives your horse a sharp tap for not responding it should be almost as natural as breathing. It obviously may take some time for you to develop this sort of almost instinctual response.

Exercise 2: Developing a Relationship Between Your Hands and Your Horse's Mouth

The simple act of your horse giving to the bit can go a long way in managing a stressful situation. When your horse is concerned about something, his ears will perk up, and his head and neck will rise. This is often the first indication that his flight instinct is being awakened. Yielding to the bit and lowering his neck again will help to relax him. The familiar exercise will help to get his mind off whatever he's scared of and back on his job. You and your mount should *both* understand the idea of giving to each other.

A horse that is trained to travel "on the bit," that is, flexed at the poll, using his back and hindquarters, is ideally prepared to begin bombproofing. However, teaching such advanced concepts is beyond the range of this publication. Further, though desirable, such schooling is really unnecessary to successfully employ the techniques that this book *does* describe. If you and your horse already have sophisticated training, that's great. It will help you immeasurably. Skip the next few paragraphs.

If your hands jolt up and down with your seat, you are accidentally giving your horse commands. It's confusing to your horse when your hands tell him something different than your legs. Although he may soon learn that tuning out your hands alto-gether is the simplest response, this comes with drawbacks. You want your horse to respond to a light touch to provide a pleasurable ride. Therefore, your hands need to be able to act independently of the rest of your body.

Besides acting independently, your hands also need to act predictably. How would you hold the hand of a friend if she had her eyes closed and you were leading her around? You'd have a connection with your friend's hand, so she wouldn't be surprised when you changed direction. You wouldn't suddenly decide to pull her in a circle. You wouldn't hold her hand loosely and then yank it when you decided to change directions. This holds true when you're riding, too. Your horse should trust your hands to act predictably.

All the joints of your arm, that is, your fingers, your elbow, and even your shoulder, should be flexible, allowing your horse to move freely ahead. The only exception is when you are trying to slow or bend him. Tensing any, or all, of these joints will cause pressure on your horse's mouth. This shouldn't be accidental. You can experiment when you're riding to see how subtle changes in your posture and the torque of your fingers can dramatically affect your animal. As you refine this process of asking your mount to yield to your hand, and then rewarding him when he does, you'll find it enables you to have a sort of conversation with his mouth.

I find that the hardest thing to teach riders is to keep the *outside* rein quiet. (By *outside* rein, I mean the rein on the outside of the horse when he is bent around in a circle, curve, or turn, the *inside* rein being the rein on the inside of the horse's bend.) This is particularly true when riding an untrained horse, because of his irregular movements. If you're unsure whether you need some help in this area, this simple test can help you decide.

Put your hands in the normal riding position just in front of his withers. Now, can you ride in control at all three gaits keeping your outside finger plastered in one spot? If you can, congratulations! However, if you find yourself giving the mane a massage with one hand, don't despair. I have an exercise that can help.

The "Hands Still" Exercise. Put a neck strap on your horse. Once you've taken a light contact with the *outside* rein, wrap your fingers around the strap. Besides providing a fix for the problem immediately, it will help to teach you what the correct position feels like. Practice circling and changing direction while you try to keep a steady, consistent contact with the *outside* rein.

Practice Using Your Inside Rein. Your *inside* rein should be used by taking up the tension and then releasing it *the moment* that you feel your horse give to you. Don't pick up more tension when he yields. Your horse has to be rewarded so he comes to understand that when he obeys, you'll allow him freedom again.

Exercise 3: Going Sideways

You'll want to be able to position your horse's front end or hind end as you please to help with your bombproofing work. Your horse should be able to travel laterally at the same time he moves forward. You should be able to ride him, in a straight line, toward something (anything—a tree, or rock, or dressage letter, if you're so inclined) with his front legs and hind legs traveling on different paths. Obviously, your horse will need to have at least a rudimentary knowledge of how to move away from leg pressure. When you push with your calf, he needs to understand that the correct response is to move away from it as the horse is doing in the drawing on page 42 (fig. 2.7).

The exercises I outline here will insure that your horse understands what you're asking when you signal him to scoot sideways. Further, they will give you more control over him, which is always better. However, the exercises play a larger part than just schooling your horse to be obedient. They will also play an important role in your riding strategy and managing your horse in stressful situations. How you position your horse in relation to scary objects will often determine if you are successful in getting by them, and his position will often determine your safety around traffic or in other treacherous situations.

Let's begin by talking about simple mechanics. I'll focus on the important basics necessary for you to steer effectively, particularly when things aren't going as planned. Many equestrians don't understand how they can direct their horses' hind ends with their reins. However, this knowledge will help you to move your horse sideways.

Though you can shift your mount's quarters over with leg pressure, you can also move them with opposing rein pressure. If you want your horse's hind end to move to the right, use left leg pressure *and* upward left rein pressure. You're using the opposing left rein correctly if you're moving that hand toward your right breast.

This may sound confusing, but here's a quick exercise you can perform unmounted to clarify how this works. While standing to the side of your horse's neck, pick up a rein and pull his nose toward you. It will promptly become obvious that his quarters will tend to shift in the opposite direction. Simply stated, pull his face left, and his bottom will go right. It is just mechanics, and it works the same way while you're on your horse's back.

This rein aid also provides an effective and rapid correction if your horse uses "backing away" as a method of resisting your request to move forward. If you quickly lift one rein, his hind end will have to move over, ending his evasive behavior.

Make sure you understand these concepts before you go on to the actual exercises listed below. This understanding will help you to instinctually do the correct thing while mounted.

Turn on the forehand is useful in many ways (fig. 2.4). It will familiarize your horse with how to move from leg pressure, and help him learn concentration and obedience. It will help *you* learn to better coordinate your hand and leg aids. As a practical maneuver, it can be employed to position your horse in tight places. Additionally, displacing his hind end is an effective behavior correction.

Before you try to perform this movement, you should know what it is, and what it looks like. Think of your horse's front and hind legs making two distinct arcs, a smaller one with his front legs, and a larger one with his hind legs.

To teach your horse this movement, start by establishing a forward, energetic walk. For clarity's sake, let's say you're traveling clockwise around the arena. Your horse's steps should be long and ground-covering. When he's moving without hesitation, make sure you have a "feel" of your horse's mouth. A "feel" doesn't imply pulling. Remember the analogy of holding hands with a friend. Next, turn your horse left, toward the wall, as if you were making a sharp turn into it.

2.4

Turn on the Forehand

The horse pivots around his inside front leg.

While the wall prevents your horse from walking forward and helps illuminate what you're asking him to do, your hands should *also* tell him that you want his front end to stop. Simultaneously, your leg—in this case, the left one—should tell him you want his back half to continue moving, so it describes a semicircle around his front end. You can also tap him behind your leg with your dressage whip to help move his quarters around.

In addition to using your leg and whip, you should also employ your left rein. Bring it up and back, toward your right breast. This will assist you in scooting your horse's hind end over.

If you're confused about *which* leg to use *when*, here's a simple method that may help you to understand. If you were standing on the ground next to your horse and you wanted him to move *right*, you'd have to push on his *left* side. You couldn't pull him in the direction that you wanted him to go. The same is true of your leg. You can't pull with it, only push. You use it the same way that you would use a hand on the ground to shove him where you want him to go.

How much leg should you use? You should already know the answer to this question, since it's always the same, no matter what exercise you're attempting. The answer is, of course, *whatever it takes*. While you don't want to "attack" your horse, since he is probably just trying to figure out what you're asking, you need to *persist* and *intensify* your aids until you begin to get the desired result. The whip will help him to understand you're asking for something. After a while, when your mount has learned what his correct response should be, he'll react to just light leg pressure.

The first time you attempt a *turn on the forehand*, it will probably look like a sharp turn into the wall, with minimal movement of your horse's hind end. However, your goal, through repetition, is to get your horse to cross his hind legs and step them gracefully around his front end.

Turn on the haunches is when your horse's front legs circle around his back legs, the opposite of what they do in the *turn on the forehand* (fig. 2.5). To teach your horse this exercise, begin by walking him along the wall clockwise. Since he'll need to shift his weight over his hindquarters to perform this movement, your next step will be to ask him to halt. This will naturally encourage your horse to balance by carrying his hind legs further under his body.

Then, ask him to back a step or two. Simultaneously, turn your horse's head away from the wall—in this case, to the right. Using a neck rein can help you position your mount correctly. If you

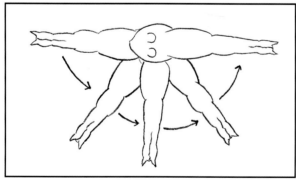

2.5

Turn on the Haunches

The horse pivots around his inside hind leg.

turn by carrying both reins to the right—whether they are in one hand or two—your horse's neck will stay straighter. This is desirable. You want both his neck and his body to be mostly straight. Simply turning his head with a direct rein will often result in his neck bulging, and ultimately, his front legs going one direction and his hind legs the other.

Your left leg behind the girth prevents his hindquarters from swinging out and your right leg at the girth encourages the horse to pivot. You can tap your horse with a dressage whip on his shoulder or neck to help him understand that he should move his front end, so he pivots around his haunches.

Head away provides a powerful tool to help you control and manage your horse under stressful conditions.

If your horse is spooking from an object, many times he can be coerced past it if you bend his head away from the object and push his quarters toward it (fig. 2.6). This is an important tactic in bombproofing. Besides being a effective way to get where you want to go, practicing it will teach your horse to obey your leg. Moving on a straight line with his feet on two tracks (or two *paths*) will supple him. As with the rest of the exercises, it will help *you* to learn to better coordinate your aids.

The idea is for your horse to move forward and sideways at the same time. For those of you who are familiar with the shoulder-in, this is a simplified version of this movement. The quickest way to teach this movement is, once again, to use the wall. The natural barricade insures that he'll move laterally from your leg pressure, instead of only shooting forward. Once he masters *head away* against the fence, he can graduate to performing it in an unconfined area.

Start this exercise by walking your horse clockwise around the arena. Make sure he's striding energetically, so you have the feeling that he's going someplace. Ride past the short side of your arena. When you get to the turn, though, keep your horse's head facing the wall in front of him. Your aim is to continue around the arena as you normally would, only with your horse looking to the outside (or toward the arena wall), instead of straight ahead. Also, your horse's hindquarters should move toward the center of the arena, so that they follow a separate track from his front legs.

To accomplish this, you need to carry both reins a bit to the right. Your left rein will act to keep your horse's head toward the wall. You'll find that slight upward pressure with this rein will assist you with moving his hind end the correct direction. When you use this upward pressure, try to hold your rein away from your horse's neck.

In the meantime, your right rein should maintain a friendly contact, so it will be there to correct your horse if he bends too much. The right amount of bend is when you can just see the corner of his left eye. When you open your right rein (turning your thumb the direction you wish to go, which in this case would be the right), it will also serve to direct your horse down the wall.

Simultaneously, apply pressure with your left leg behind the girth to scoot his hind end over. If a squeeze doesn't work, don't be afraid to increase your aid to a tap with the whip or even a vigorous kick. A dull horse may need to be tapped to inspire him, while a more sensitive one will only need a hint of calf pressure. It's your job to adjust your aids according to what your horse needs.

2.6
Head Away

Leg-yielding is another great exercise to supple your horse (fig. 2.7). It, like *head away*, also involves him traveling forward and laterally at the same time. However, he'll be positioned a bit differently in this movement. When viewed from above, a horse leg-yielding diagonally across the arena travels with his body and head remaining parallel to the long sides of the arena. Your horse will have a bend around your leg, and he'll look away from the direction he's traveling. To accomplish this, his legs need to cross.

The simplest way to teach this movement is on the circle. Let's say you're riding clockwise around it. Starting in the walk, decrease your circle until it's fairly small—ten feet around or so. It should be as small as you can make it while comfortably maintaining a forward gait. Then, while you continue to walk, encourage your horse to enlarge the circle with a few steps of *leg-yielding*.

Both of your hands can move the direction you want to go—in this case, to the left. Your horse should stay looking a bit to the right, just the way you would want him if you remained on the same circle. Your right leg will be the more active one, because its job is to push your horse's quarters to the left. As always, it will need to lend as much motivation as needed to get some results. In addition, you should always be ready to support your leg aids with a reminder from your dressage whip.

I find most horses are willing to fade to the outside, because a bigger circle is less work for them. It's almost as if you have gravity on your side, helping you teach your horse.

The most common evasion used by horses being taught this exercise is to merely bend their necks excessively and move their shoulders out on the circle, since "neck-yielding" is definitely an easier option than leg- yielding! The way to thwart this is to insist that your horse remain only slightly bent in his neck. The same guidelines that helped you determine the correct amount of bend for *head away* can be used for *leg-yielding*. If you can just see the corner of your mount's eye, you have it about right. However, if you can see the whole side of his face, you need to make sure that you're using both reins as a pair, not merely the inside one.

Once you can do this, you can try *leg-yielding* back onto a smaller circle. To introduce *leg-yielding* on a straight line, ride down the quarter line and then push your horse toward the outside of the arena. Your aids will be the same as those used on the circle, as will the evasions that you encounter. You'll need to focus on keeping your horse mostly straight in his head and neck, so that he responds to your leg pressure by moving sideways (therefore, crossing his legs). Riding these different variations of *leg-yielding* will greatly increase your horse's obedience and your own skill level.

If you're having lots of trouble (or if your horse is), resume work on the *turn on the forehand*. Executed properly, it will get his rear legs to cross, and that's half the goal of *leg-yielding*. Once your mount has mastered it, you'll both find coming back to this exercise easier.

Exercise 4: Neck-Reining

This skill is practical, useful, and absolutely necessary for mounted police work. Your horse needs to have *some* understanding of how to *neck-rein*, or you won't be able to ride with one hand. As a tool to deal with real-world circumstances, it's hard to beat.

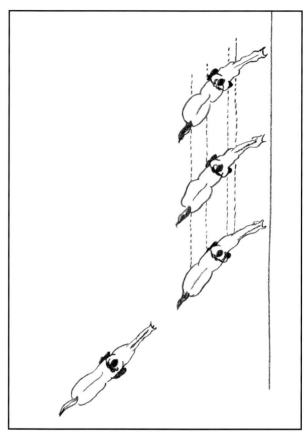

2.7
Leg-Yield

Neck-reining improves your horse's versatility and control and can also help you to perform lateral movements. This is true even for English riders. The horses we use in police work perform basic dressage movements, and learning to *neck-rein* hasn't hurt them a bit.

To train your horse to *neck-rein*, start walking him in a circle. Your reins can remain in both hands. Then, change direction, let's say to the left. First, use a direct leading rein on the left side (to use the left direct rein, you'll "hitchhike" with your left hand, the thumb turned the direction you want to go). In addition to using the left leading rein, press your right rein against your horse's neck—slightly higher than you would normally do on a trained horse. Remember, this is a training exercise. You don't have to look pretty.

Hopefully, after repeated turns, your horse will start to understand that the two rein aids mean the same thing: he should turn left. If he's having trouble absorbing this, you can use a dressage whip on your mount's neck to back up your rein aid. Simply press or tap him on the neck with it (on the right side, if you're turning to the left). It may help him start to understand that the desired response is to move away from the rein pressure—and that nasty whip.

Remember to initially make big circles and changes of direction. Once your horse grasps that if he turns, you'll only barely touch him on the neck, he'll willingly comply. Eventually, you'll stop utilizing the leading rein when you ask for the *neck-rein*.

If your horse is having a problem figuring out the new lesson, sometimes crossing the reins underneath his neck will assist him in understanding. It's a quick and effective way to train him to *neck-rein* and usually, you can start right away with one-hand riding. However, I need to interject a few words of caution: If you employ this method, you'll want to have a ground person with you. Otherwise, if your horse panics, you may find you have no control whatsoever. Obviously, this is a schooling exercise, to be used in a restricted situation. Crossing your reins prior to hacking out your skittish three-year-old might not be prudent.

The way to cross your reins is simple. Just take the rein that's attached to the *left* side of your horse's bit, and wrap it under his neck, so it comes out on the *right* side of his withers. When you ride your horse, you'll have your right rein in your left hand, and the left rein in your right hand. With the reins fixed this way, whenever you use a right neck rein,

the bit will simultaneously tug on the left side of his mouth. Of course, the reverse is true as well.

This "rigged" bridle will do the teaching. Your job is to circle and turn, so it has a chance to work. Don't forget to go easy on your aids and perform sweeping turns. Your ground person should walk next to your horse, and follow every direction change until you're comfortable.

While English riders often hesitate to teach *neck-reining*, Western riders are often similarly allergic to holding the reins in both hands. It's as if they are paralyzed on one side. However, just as *neck-reining* has its benefits, so does riding two-handed. Many of the exercises listed in this chapter will be difficult, if not impossible, to teach your mount when riding with only one hand.

Learning to Develop a "Feel"

No one would argue that your position in the saddle is not important, because it forms the foundation on which all of your riding skills will be built. However, your skills as a horseman and trainer will also largely depend on your ability to "think like a horse."

Rather than only focusing narrowly on particular skills, to get the best performance, you'll need to *learn to trust your "feel"*—to act instinctively, and adapt immediately. Make no mistake, you are learning and perfecting a sports skill, but a sports skill that is complicated by the fact that another living creature has been mixed into the equation. Don't become so analytical that you lose sight of developing your gut reactions. Developing a feel for what your animal is doing will take time, but, through trial and error, you'll become more efficient and skilled.

Sometimes your horse will relax if you allow him a moment to assess a spooky object. He has every intention of obeying you, but he just wants to take a gander. Other times, though, when he's peeking at something frightening, he's only waiting for a sign of weakness from you to garner the courage to be disobedient.

You have to be quick to decide what course of action to take. You may have to re-evaluate that decision and pick another tactic, again all in a matter of seconds. Don't be afraid to listen to what your subconscious tells you. Your horse will probably inform you if your decision was incorrect.

When I teach new mounted officers, watching them struggle to control their own positions, and their ineffectual attempts to manage—much less correct—their horses, I'm reminded how difficult learning to ride really is. None of us like to admit fault, but when you can't get your horse to do what you've requested, honestly examining your effectiveness and reactions is vital.

Are you sure you were paying attention to the signals your mount was sending you? Were you ignoring the times your horse disregarded your attempt to push him a bit faster? Could you have been a little more insistent with your aids? Could you have been braver and more sure of yourself?

In *any* trying instance, it's important to remember to keep your aids on the horse. This means sufficient rein and leg contact. Being prepared, coupled with a strong mental attitude, will often make the difference between a successful or unsuccessful outcome. If your own concentration and resolve fail you, it's almost impossible to keep your horse on task.

Many times riders insist that they're doing everything right, but between bad timing, technique, and a lack of training, the horse manages to evade the rider's request. Success or failure can be related to very subtle changes.

Given enough time and effort, though, the rider will begin to act—and react—appropriately. With solid skills and techniques as a foundation, he'll be able to do more than perch on his horse's back, praying for things to be better. Then he'll begin to enjoy success.

The Round Pen and Longeing

Since they are so fashionable, I should mention the *roundpen* training systems. While I love to use a round pen for schooling green horses, it's not a major part of my program. However, many of the popular "bitless" breaking systems center around its use. The round pen *can* be used to habituate your horse to some types of obstacles, but for bombproofing work, I find it ultimately too limiting. Nevertheless, it can be usefully employed, particularly when your horse is barely broken.

When longeing an uneducated animal, the outside wall thwarts the common evasion of running sideways, so it's much easier to keep him circling correctly. Also, besides compelling him to be obedient, the walls of a round pen serve to block out distractions that a young horse may find overwhelming. His body and brain both need to learn to focus on their jobs—that is, to do as you wish.

Riding your mount in the round pen can be beneficial for the same reasons. Oftentimes, in a large arena situation, the green horse's circles will become more egg-shaped when he nears the arena exit because he wants to leave. It's amazing how an animal can so quickly fathom where the nearest exit is located!

The round pen will help enforce your outside aids. When your horse is better schooled to listen to them, your outside leg and rein will serve the same purpose as the pen's walls. In the meantime, the walls will keep him straight on the circle. When riding in a round pen, your horse may slow at the gate—but at least that's easy to correct.

Once basic obedience has been established as a routine, however, the round pen plays little, if any, part in bombproofing. The same is true of *longeing*. If I have a horse that is already schooled and goes well, I don't waste much time on it. I don't mean to imply that longeing isn't useful, merely that it doesn't play a large role in bombproofing your mount.

Longeing *does* develop submission in your horse. It can also help him to learn voice commands. Finally, it may serve to improve and develop his gaits. Mostly, I like to use it with green horses, but I also find it useful for retraining the spoiled horse. Some horses arrive at our police horse barn with absolutely no manners at all. Even if a horse like this has been well-schooled under saddle, I'll put him on the longe line to teach compliance and respect. Besides instilling these assets, green horses further benefit: Not only does longeing tend to improve their suppleness, and therefore their gaits, it also helps them find the balance to improve their transitions.

The lessons taught on the longe most definitely transfer to work under saddle. Once your horse's acquiescence and steadiness have improved there, you'll find him more willing to work for you in general. If you think your horse could use some polish in these basic areas, find an instructor to help you, and pick up one of the excellent books devoted entirely to the subject. If you think your horse could use some polish in these basic areas, find an instructor to help you, and pick up one of the excellent books devoted entirely to the subject: *All About Lungeing* by Paul Fielder, *The Art of Lungeing* by Sylvia Stanier, and *Lungeing and Long-Reining* by Jennie Loriston-Clarke are a few.

CHAPTER 3

Bombproofing Concepts

You will need two types of skills in order to be able to bombproof successfully: a conceptual understanding of how your horse thinks, and specific strategies to actually bombproof your horse.

Basic Instincts

Understanding how your horse thinks is the foundation for all of the strategies that I will suggest to you. If you understand your horse's motivation, it will be easier to comprehend why certain training methods are effective, while others are not. *All horses have the same basic instincts,* though they undeniably vary in intensity with each individual.

Imagine yourself back in the scenario mentioned at the beginning of this book. You are hacking toward your friend's house, preoccupied with removing bits of hay from your gloves, when your horse spots the tent a neighbor's child has set up. It's windy, and the roof of the tent billows. Your horse jolts to a stop, and he wheels and launches himself in the opposite direction. As you struggle to haul him back under control, thoughts roll through your mind. *Stupid horse! He nearly ran us right into that tree. He has the brain of a hamster.*

Your horse, of course, considers the scenario described above in another way. He *saw* the tent shuddering, waiting to spring toward him and swallow him whole, and supposes it was his quick reaction that saved his skin (since *you* obviously were dozing and failed to note the danger).

You and your horse are both doing what comes naturally. You're thinking like a human being, and he's thinking like a horse. The point? He's not going to start thinking like a human being, not now, not next week, not ever. It's up to *you* to try and understand the way *his* mind works.

If you understand your horse's motivation, it will be easier to comprehend why certain training methods are effective, while others are not.

Here are the most common equine instincts:

The Flight Instinct

A horse will attempt to flee predators. He tries to escape when he's frightened, using his speed to outpace danger. This strategy worked as a survival mechanism for wild equines. This is ingrained behavior, genetic, as much a part of your horse as his legs or tail.

When you attempt to control your animal's flight, your horse, in essence, reacts by fighting for his life. He rears, bucks, shies, or bolts away from the hazard. The undesirable behavior that the horse exhibits is his struggle to convince his rider that he needs to disappear from the area.

The Victim Instinct

So why *did* your horse suppose that the tent might eat him? As I mentioned earlier, it's because for a billion years, horses have been prey, like deer or rabbits, instead of predators, like wolves and cougars. An equine's survival often hinged on his ability to notice a predator and bolt away from it before it had a chance to jump on his withers.

The Herd Instinct

Your horse will always have the instinct to stay close to his equine friends. Herd instinct is what makes him "scream" when he's in the horse trailer or barn (or anyplace he may not be secure) without the presence of nearby buddies to reassure him. Herd instinct is what makes him hurry along the trail when he's behind the other horses, or what inspires him to leap over a stream he's afraid of in order to stay with them. Though every horse comes complete

with herd instinct, the strength of the trait varies greatly from horse to horse. It may impact your horse's character tremendously, or barely at all.

This behavior also developed as a survival mechanism. In the wild, stragglers that lollygagged behind the group were prone to be eaten—something that tended to happen to the sick, old, or very young. A healthy animal was sure to be careful that he wasn't far from his pals.

Your Horse's Vision

Although it's not really an "instinct," how your horse *sees* the objects around him will affect his behavior. The reason he suddenly decides a particular rock looks frightening may well be because he sees differently than you do—*not* because he's trying to make you insane. Have you ever seen a cat or a dog chase objects on a television? Your horse can't recognize that kind of three-dimensional detail. His eyes see two different pictures at once because of how they're situated.

Your horse doesn't see as acutely as you do, either. A horse sees in black and white, mingled with shades of gray. If you keep this in mind, you will have a lot more respect for a horse's ability (and willingness) to jump obstacles you put before him.

Keep these basic equine instincts in mind as I discuss the basic strategies and techniques you need to bombproof your horse. These are divided into four sections:

1. The Comfort Zone, Working through the Reaction, and Repetition

2. Proactive vs. Reactive Skills

3. Punishment and Reward

4. Testing within Training

Section 1
The Comfort Zone, Working through the Reaction, and Repetition

A. The Comfort Zone

When your horse lopes around the same small course of fences that he has negotiated a hundred times, he's well within his *comfort zone*. On the other hand, when a green, three-year-old, never-seen-anything baby is asked to leap a log into water, he has been pushed far out of his *comfort zone*. As far as he's concerned, you've asked him to do something impossible, and he doesn't like it.

Whenever you train your horse to another level by introducing a new stimulus, you need to find the boundary, or edge, of his *comfort zone*, and push him to stretch a bit beyond it. You need to "tread the line" and find the right balance just beyond the place where he remains relaxed but before the place where he is totally uncomfortable. This "breaching" of the boundary of his *comfort zone* is what gets him closer to accepting a new stimulus, which in turn takes him to the next level of training. The process is repeated until the stimulus is no longer a concern and the horse has accepted his task. Not breaching this boundary (and thereby avoiding conflict), or asking him for so much that the task is impossible, gives you the same result—you teach your horse nothing! This is true whether you are working on counter-canter, or merely trying to get him to stroll down a road.

Of course, this is a very personal thing, unique to each individual animal and circumstance. What constitutes a minor test of nerve and obedience for one horse, may be an insurmountable obstacle to the next. It depends on the horse's natural aptitude, coupled with his experience level and prior training.

Jumping larger fences might test a novice level event horse. For the horse that has never jumped, striding over a pole on the ground may be challenge enough. Taking the lead on a trail ride might stretch the boundary for another. The examples of what might be testing for any individual are almost endless.

The *comfort zone* boundary can also be physically established by distancing a horse from a threat. Usually, when a horse flees, he assesses the risk by glancing backward while he sprints. Eventually, he stops galloping. He's calculated that he's out of danger. He may have traveled twenty feet or more than a hundred yards, but right then, he has reached his *comfort zone*.

Imagine a noisy machine working—like a bulldozer. If it is clanking around right next to your horse, the noise will probably upset him. But will he flinch at the sound when it's several blocks away? Probably not. Somewhere in between these extremes is the boundary of your horse's *comfort zone*. When you work to gradually increase the size of the *comfort zone* of your horse to anything—from sudden loud noises, to rocks on the ground, to cars whizzing by—you are sensory training your horse.

Think about this concept and try to imagine how things appear to your horse. When you decide which route to take in crossing a ditch, consider whether your horse can tackle a steep bank, or will a flat, open crossing amply challenge him? The idea is to ask questions, but only ones that your horse can reasonably answer successfully.

So how do *you* decide what is an appropriate question for *your* horse? The key to your success is that you must have a probable positive outcome. A positive outcome first means that you can actually get your horse to do what you ask, and second, that the experience will build confidence in him. If you have reasonable expectations of meeting these criteria, then the task you are asking is appropriate.

When I ask a horse in one of my clinics to cross a mattress (something I do, regularly), chances are I have pushed him well out of his *comfort zone*. The horse will almost certainly be at least mildly alarmed, and he may well back-up, spin, or try to bolt and leave entirely. He may even rear. However, in this case, the flustered horse is not indicating that I have asked him too much. In this kind of controlled, clinic environment, one way or another, it's a pretty sure bet that eventually, the animal will see things my way and attempt the crossing.

Now, if *you* aren't an experienced rider, and you plunk down a mattress in your field and ask your mount to cross it, you might not be so sure of the exercise's outcome. If you don't possess the knowledge or equipment to work your horse from the ground, and you haven't the foresight to bring a friend to help you, your horse may *not* be easily coerced into cooperating. If he refuses to traverse the mattress, and you don't have the tools to insist on his obedience, all you are successfully teaching your horse is that he doesn't need to obey you in all instances. Obviously, if you can't get your horse to do as you are asking, this can't be considered a positive outcome.

The second part of determining if the question you're asking your horse is appropriate, is whether it will result in a confidence-building experience. Let's use the example of the mattress again. If I'm successful in getting my horse to cross the mattress (as I will be, in a well organized situation), there's almost no chance that the experience *won't* create assurance. The mattress won't actually spring into the air and "bite" my horse on the fetlock; it won't trap his feet or hurt him. He'll end up on the other side of it, alive, and intact. I haven't "lied." In other words, I haven't asked him to perform a task that

might indeed be harmful to him. Once he has repeated the task enough times, he'll start to grasp that nothing terrible is happening to him. Then, he'll begin to graciously comply, and also relax.

However, if I "lie" to my mount, the opposite is true. To give you another example, if I ask my horse to ford a stream that has a drop-off that suddenly plunges him into water past his withers, or has a muddy bottom that trips him, the "dullest" of creatures will rapidly absorb the fact that the person astride his back is not to be believed. If I ask my horse to leap a fence that's beyond his scope, and he's unsuccessful in clearing it, all I've demonstrated is that he should use his own judgment to decide which obstacles he should attempt, and that he should be prepared to refuse any task that seems questionable. In these kinds of circumstances, I'm training my horse, very effectively, to *not* obey.

B. Working through the Reaction

Once you *breach your horse's comfort zone boundary*, he'll react by rearing, bucking, shying, trembling, and so forth. He's showing you that he's frightened, resistant, or both. It's now necessary to *work through the reaction*.

In order to manage the situation effectively, you need to employ all the basic skills outlined in Chapter Two. I'm going to build on those skills in subsequent chapters, so you'll be comfortable and confident when the going gets rough. By way of example: if your horse refuses to go forward, you can push him in circles until he obeys your leg. Or, you can use his *herd instinct* to help you, and let him follow another horse. If all else fails, you can school him from the ground (see Chapter Five, *Working Your Horse from the Ground*).

One aspect that I cover in more detail in upcoming chapters is how you also need to acquire control over *your* reaction. When your horse pivots and heads for home, you have to instinctively know what to do. A rider who hesitates and allows her horse to feel her own apprehension and fear may frighten him even more, so you need to practice until the correct reaction is instinctive.

C. Repetition

Repetition is the glue that makes the lessons stick. Let's go back to the example of the mattress one last time. The first time he crosses it, your horse is still liable to be frightened. He'll probably jump over the last half of the mattress and may land running. He may act as if he thinks that he was merely lucky to have lived through the single attempt. Even if you've done everything right, this one (probably ragged) crossing likely hasn't totally convinced him that the obstacle is safe. Be aware that even if a horse calmly walks over an object several times, he may not have fully absorbed the exercise. Sometimes, a horse can be completely habituated to a new object or task in one lesson, and other times, he'll need the lesson repeated on subsequent days before it is really taken in. For example, a sensible horse may accept all water obstacles or all logs on the ground after schooling over a single stream or log. However, the spooky, high-strung horse may also need to negotiate *different* logs or *other* water obstacles before you can consider him habituated to these things.

In both cases, repetition is what convinces the horse that whatever you're asking him to do isn't harmful. Once your horse negotiates an obstacle (or accomplishes a new skill) without harm or punishment, he will be more willing to try it again. The horse performs a little better each time, and therefore, his assurance and obedience grows.

The photographs on pages 53 through 59 demonstrate the entire bombproofing process using a mattress and clearly show how the progression works. A horse that starts out extremely worried and concerned even about stepping over the mattress, will, through repetition, learn to walk comfortably over it with his rider on his back.

I start by testing to find the horse's *comfort zone*, proceed to work on the ground, then progress to work under saddle. During the process, I use many strategies that you'll be reading about in upcoming pages: manipulating the obstacle, approaching the obstacle, ground safety considerations, and effective equipment. I also consider the knowledge that the rider has of the horse. The series of pictures shows how to work through the horse's reaction while breaching the upper boundary of his *comfort zone* and performing the necessary repetition to adequately habituate him.

I started this horse out by testing him with the rider on board. The rider knew that this four-year-old Thoroughbred-paint cross would probably jump the mattress, and would probably buck, as well. She approached the mattress to attempt to cross it, but the horse would not even come close enough to attempt it. Rather than argue with him and risk her safety, she dismounted and worked the horse from the ground. Remember, this is a training session—time, patience, and progression work much better than force. Photo 3.1 shows the horse looking at the obstacle. Notice that I manipulate this obstacle by asking the horse to cross it at the easiest—that is, narrowest—point.

After the rider dismounted, we put on a Monty Roberts Dually Halter™ that has a moveable caves-son that tightens when the horse backs-up or retreats, thus encouraging forward movement. If the horse backs-up or evades, his action—not the rider's—will create tension on his nose, and forward movement will create a release. You can see this halter in Photo 3.2 where I'm immediately praising the horse for moving forward. (For more on fitting and using this halter, see Chapter Five, *Working Your Horse from the Ground*, p. 77). This way, the horse will quickly learn that if he does what I ask, he'll be rewarded, and if he makes the wrong decision, it is his decision and not mine. When he rushed or jumped toward me, I raised my hand up toward his face to keep him from stepping or jumping on me. Be careful not to actually touch the horse in this circumstance—you don't want to confuse touching him with punishment. Use the hand to facilitate his seeing that you are in his path.

I also used a longe line, so I could safely keep out of the horse's way. Once the horse decided to cross the obstacle, he would probably jump it, and I wanted him to have space to do so without jumping on top of me. Other safety considerations were putting the stirrups up so they did not flail about, and getting the reins out of the way. In this case, I've doubled them around his neck. Keep in mind that this ground technique requires a certain amount of dexterity and finesse. It is necessary to keep the longe line in one hand and not dangle it, or you will get tangled. You must also be able to move quickly—to get out of the way, if necessary. Finally, you may need a certain amount of strength, because if the horse retreats suddenly, you must hold the line firmly but with enough finesse to know when to move back with the horse (photo 3.3). I discuss working your horse from the ground in a great deal more detail in Chapter Five.

Photo 3.4 shows the horse being tested in hand. To start, your goal is to get the horse close enough to sniff and then touch the mattress. At this point, he would not come close enough to sniff it. Instead, I simply encouraged him to go forward toward it. He walked to each side. Photo 3.5 shows

him trying to find a way around the mattress. Photo 3.6 shows—after many repetitions—the horse getting near enough to put a foot on it. Now he knows that the mattress is okay and will not hurt him.

I continued working the horse, but he still found ways to walk around and avoid stepping on the mattress. It was time to manipulate the obstacle to encourage him more. I placed poles on each side of the mattress to keep the horse focused and to create a barrier to help prevent him from running out to the sides. I could have also placed one side of the mattress against a wall or fence, or added cones, a ground pole, or barriers on the other side. Sometimes I use two mattresses, laid end to end, which create a much longer obstacle that is difficult to walk around. With two mattresses, it is also possible to create a narrow space between them to walk through. This narrow space encourages the horse to eventually step onto the mattress.

In Photo 3.7, the horse evaluated the situation by sniffing the mattress, and in 3.8, he finally went across—albeit a little obliquely over the pole. However, in the next few pictures, he jumped over the mattress itself, getting calmer each time, and I worked closer to him. Keep the horse on task—do not let him get far away from the obstacle during this phase. As soon as the horse landed, I asked him to turn around immediately and try the mattress again, from the opposite side. He probably jumped this about a dozen times!

In Photo 3.16, the rider remounted, and I started the horse forward by guiding him with the cheek piece. I did not want to hold the reins, because the rider needs to be able to control the horse. He was, by now, confident with me leading, so it made sense to build from there. As you can see, we continued to reinforce the repetition as the horse gradually went more confidently, and by the

3.1—3.22
The Mattress Obstacle

3.1

I make the decision to work Jasper in hand and lead him up to the mattress.

3.2

After asking Jasper to make a few approaches to the mattress, I reward him with a pat for his attempts to obey my instructions.

3.3

When I ask him to cross the mattress, Jasper starts backing-up. I keep a tight hold on the longe line. This causes the halter to tighten on Jasper's nose, and he quickly learns that forward movement eases the pressure.

3.4

Rather than backing-up, Jasper evades the mattress by running out to the side, avoiding it completely.

3.5

He tries again to avoid the mattress by running around it. Notice how I keep my distance and my eye on Jasper's body language.

3.6

Patience and repetition begin to pay off. Jasper has finally touched the mattress. He receives another reward—a pat and rub on the neck.

3.7

He has been trying to run around the mattress, so two ground poles are placed on each side to encourage passage over the mattress. Here, he is allowed to sniff and explore. Again, patience is needed to give Jasper time to accept his task.

3.8

Jasper still wants to run around the mattress, so he jumps the ground poles. Keep a good distance from the horse as I am doing, so he doesn't jump on top of you.

3.9

Another good reason to keep distance between you and your horse while training: Here, he performs quite a leap over the side of the mattress.

3.10

I'm ready to get out of the way. As soon as he gets back on the ground, I ask him to turn around and try the mattress again from the other side. Don't let the horse get too far away from the obstacle before asking for a repetition.

3.11

Although he is still jumping over the mattress, he has calmed down quite a bit. I'm able to work closer to him.

3.12

Now Jasper is just hopping over mattress. Notice how I'm ready to immediately turn him around to cross again.

3.13

Here, Jasper's front hoof touches the mattress as he cross it. He receives a big reward for his effort.

3.14

He's finally crossed the mattress by stepping on, rather than jumping over it.

3.15

Jasper now realizes that the mattress is not a monster and he walks over it with ease. We keep repeating this until he's almost bored.

3.16

Now that Jasper is calmly walking on the mattress, it's time to get his rider up and see if he can confidently carry them both over at the walk. Asking him to do this will breach the comfort zone once again. I lead him to the mattress. Although Lisa is in control of the reins, I hold the cheek piece of the bridle to give Jasper extra confidence.

3.16

end, the rider could calmly take the horse over the mattress completely unassisted, with no jumping or bucking (photos 3.17 to 3.22).

Section 2
Proactive vs. Reactive Skills

Management skills can be used in either a *proactive* or *reactive* manner. When you *anticipate* a potential problem and try to thwart it, this is considered *proactive riding*.

I'll give you an example. Let's imagine you and your horse are out on a trail ride. As you hack by your neighbor's field, you notice he has acquired several new pets—*llamas*! You don't wait for your horse to spot the animals. Instead, you immediately ask him to concentrate on his job. You bend him in the opposite direction of the llamas and ask for a

few steps of *head away*. In the meantime, you push him forward into an energetic trot.

Since your horse is busy yielding to the bit and your leg, he never even sees the llamas. As a result, he remains relaxed and is past the potential problem in no time. Any quivering, running sideways, and spooking that might have occurred have been averted, due to your speedy thinking and reactions. You have *prevented* a dilemma from occurring, using *proactive* skills.

A *reactive* skill is when you *take action in response* to something that has already happened. Let's use the same scenario to demonstrate how this might work. Let's say you don't notice the new arrivals. You're busy thinking about how nice it is to have escaped the office and how wonderful it is to enjoy the day with your horse.

3.17

Jasper's first attempt with his rider results in a small hop over the mattress.

3.18

He has quieted down. I walk next to him to build more confidence.

3.19

Don't forget to work on both sides of the horse and both directions of the obstacle. Repeat, and repeat some more! Some horses need more than others.

3.20 to 3.22

Jasper now has the confidence to work the mattress obstacle without me walking next to him. Lisa will repeat this exercise many times and in both directions. He has had a successful training session, and when asked to walk over the mattress later in the day, he had no problem with it.

The first indication that something is wrong is the ugly sensation that your horse has vanished from underneath you, and the saddle is nowhere near your bottom. You grab at the air and manage to find a piece of leather (which later, proves to be the pommel). You cling to it as your horse plummets backward. Though you somehow manage to stay aboard, your horse's confidence has been shattered—not to mention *yours*. He refuses to go toward the pasture, and plants his hooves in the grass. He's shaking, and his eyes are as big as apples.

But you need to get him by the pasture. It's the only way out to the trail, and besides, he's supposed to do what you say.

It's now time to employ your *reactive* skills. Since he won't move in a straight line, you turn him in a circle, and kick him with your heels until he bounds forward. Then you straighten him and ask him to edge by the field again. Although it takes a couple of tries, your stern reminder to respond to your leg works. Your horse, though still afraid, trots by the llamas. You have used a *reactive* skill to *correct* your horse's behavior.

You might well use the same exercise to prevent a problem as you would to correct it, but it's important to recognize the difference between the two situations. I'll explain the various—and exact—solutions I use to rectify or thwart undesirable behavior later in the book.

Section 3
Punishment and Reward

It's crucial to master how to dole out both punishment and reward correctly. Punishment is hardly a popular word, but I'm not talking about beating or harming your horse. Your role will be to show your horse the path of least resistance—you'll be teaching your horse that there are consequences for his behavior. If he's acting unacceptably, there will be a consequence: your job is to make this behavior an uncomfortable option.

Let's say you're riding down a path. You arrive at a puddle. Your horse stops, wishing you'd get the message that a large body of water is blocking his way. When you fail to respond in the desired manner (turning and hacking back toward home), he tugs his head sideways, trying to jolt you into sensibility.

The most passive way to deal with this dilemma is to simply use your legs and hands to keep him facing the puddle, and hope he decides it's safe on his own. More than likely, though, that won't be enough. You progress to using leg pressure, and, if that doesn't work, then your spurs. If he still refuses to traverse the puddle, you tap him with your whip. (Although it's a good idea to keep him moving forward, to spur and whip him as soon as *you* spot the water crossing, before he has even slowed down, is patently unfair. He has the right to demonstrate his willingness before he gets jabbed in the barrel.)

Your training technique may be as simple as riding in a figure eight and pressing your spurs into his sides when he refuses to go forward, but you need to have *some* method of making it unpleasant for him when he is disobedient. This is true in all circumstances where the object is to teach. When he walks on top of you, he needs an elbow in his side or a bump on his nose with a chain. When he saunters off as you mount, the bit needs to jiggle in his mouth. Remember, your horse isn't a small child. He's a powerful animal that needs to learn respect for you, and also learn that for his every action, there is a corresponding reaction on your part. Here's the point of this example: *Whenever your horse is hesitant to do what you want, he needs to understand that he has more than one option.* He can decide to do as you ask (advance over the puddle) or be offered an unpleasant alternative (get poked in the side or stung on the bottom). When he *does* proceed, not only does he become more comfortable, but he is also reassured by the positive experience of tackling the obstacle with no ill effects, unless of course, you've asked him an unfair question like the example I mentioned on page 50.

If you discipline out of anger, punishment escalates to cruelty. Certainly, many of us have become frustrated at this point, but if you're hitting because *you're just so mad,* you need to dismount and cool down. Cruelty is never an appropriate response for the rider, and has no part in the bombproofing plan. You are attempting to alter your equine's behavior and turn his negative response into a positive one. The horse must feel that *you are his friend.* You are his relief. You are the one who will praise him and make a big fuss when he does well. He has to understand that his adverse actions caused the problem, not you.

Of course, you'll praise him for doing your bidding, as well. Always reward him immediately for a positive response with a pat on the withers or at least a word of encouragement. When you reward your horse for positive responses, he'll respond to you more quickly with every request. Once you establish this trust and bond, he'll be more willing to do as you ask.

Becoming aware of your horse's psychological makeup will help you make decisions about his training. You need to develop patience, if you don't already possess it, and riding skills, as well. You need to understand that your horse should have the time to assess a situation and try to solve his dilemma. When your horse chooses the correct path, he will be rewarded. In his mind, it will be *his* choice.

Section 4
Testing within Training

When you ask your horse to prove to you that he has actually absorbed his lessons, you're *testing* him. Although *testing is* a form of training, it differs, too. When you *test* your horse, you press his *comfort zone.* In a training environment, this is called a "self test." *Self-testing* is an instance where you try to push your horse to a new level by experimenting with questions and attempting to work him through the situation. (I'll discuss *real-life testing* later in this section.)

You should do *self-testing* regularly to note progress, and to help determine if your horse has advanced to a new level or performs a skill to an acceptable level. By training and then *testing* new limits, you'll break through to higher levels. Of course, *self-testing* must be done progressively and systematically, just as training is. Your horse should only be asked to attempt tasks where you can reasonably expect success.

Another form of *testing* that presses your horse further is when you *self-test* him with *maximum intensity.* Suppose you have been training your horse over a period of time to jump cross-country obstacles. Although you usually show him each new fence before you jump it, you set up a different situation. Your plan is to gallop a small course, without giving your horse the luxury of being shown the problems first. This *test* will ask him if he's absorbed the fact that he has to jump whatever fence he's presented with, whether or not he's been shown it beforehand. This is a new situation for him.

You ride your horse through each circumstance—in this case, toward each new fence—using skills acquired in training. In this instance, your horse will be asked to respond to your driving aids by going forward, just as he has learned in previous sessions (*even* if he thinks the new fences might be little dangerous). Your *own* training will help you react quickly whenever you feel him change his rhythm, instead of waiting for the trouble to get worse. Your skills and timing will reassure your animal. When he hesitates, he'll feel your leg against his barrel as solid as a rock on the ground. Your technique will keep you from collapsing on his mane whenever he shifts his balance.

Self-testing with *maximum-intensity* varies, of course, depending on a horse's level of training. A more schooled horse wouldn't be fazed by many tasks a "greenie" would find daunting. The problems also vary depending on the riding discipline. An appropriate challenge for an intermediate event horse might be a corner-to-corner obstacle, while a green Thoroughbred off the track might be as challenged by a trek through a small creek without a lead horse.

If it becomes obvious you've asked too much—the intermediate eventer tries to run out on the second corner, bangs his legs, suffers a meltdown—you'll probably need to make the lesson easier. You could change the second obstacle into a vertical, instead of a corner, or you could simply lower the corner or make it narrower.

How your horse responds will tell you if you need to spend more time schooling before trying the more difficult obstacle again. If he acts as if he has obviously been frightened—he swaps leads in front of the vertical you've set, and it takes him ten leaps back and forth over it before he starts to jump in good form again, this is his way of saying he has been over-faced. *Listen* to him. You need to do more homework before progressing.

However, if your horse quickly grasps the problem when you present it in an easier form—perhaps he wobbles the first time into the vertical, but then is perfect the next time and doesn't seem slightly

stressed—a small confidence booster was obviously all the help he needed. It's now reasonable to assume you might attempt the more difficult obstacle again.

The accompanying photographs show a rider as she tried to determine how close she could comfortably come to the umbrella and balloons. She began by working at a fair distance from the obstacle, and then, using *head-away* and the other techniques I discussed earlier, soon had her horse successfully passing the obstacle (photos 3.23 to 3.28).

Real-life testing is when you confront your horse with bigger challenges in circumstances that you cannot always control. Let's say you've spent time working your horse on rural roads and in light traffic where your chances of being squashed by a bus were somewhat diminished, and your horse has learned to ignore the roar of the engines and concentrate on your commands. Now, it's the moment for the genuine article.

You've planned a ride through a town or city with all of its inherent sounds, distractions, and heavy traffic. This isn't a decision you've taken lightly. Your horse seems to be informing you he's prepared. His confidence has grown to the point where he doesn't emit a snort when a motorcycle screeches by only a few feet away. He's also been obeying your commands lately, even when the wind is gusting and the days are cool.

You feel ready for the challenge, too. You've practiced your reactions. Your response to your horse's spooking is almost as instinctual as swatting a fly that's stinging you—you sink in the saddle, clomp on your leg, and then push him into shoulder-in. You almost never curl into the fetal position on his neck, either, even when a truck blasts its horn. That's good, because the pressure will be on.

The main difference between *self-testing* and *real-life testing* is that you can't manipulate the

3.23—3.28
Testing and Working in the Comfort Zone

3.23 & 3.24

Here the rider is testing Jasper to find the limit of his comfort zone. Training begins when the horse is a comfortable distance away from the obstacle.

3.25

Once you've established a horse's comfort zone, work within it until you feel that he is ready to move closer to the obstacle.

3.23—3.28 cont.
Testing and Working in the Comfort Zone

3.26

Jasper is closer, and out of his comfort zone.

3.27

Jasper is being worked using the head-away position. When he becomes comfortable at this distance from the obstacle, he is asked again to move closer.

3.28

Using the head-away again, Jasper now passes even closer to the umbrella and balloons—without any problem.

situation in the latter. Once you're there, you have little control over the conditions. You have no power over the ambulance that comes screaming down the street. You can't lean over and yell, "Pardon me, sir, but you're scaring my horse." In a *self-test* you can always lower your expectations. You can make the lesson easier. You can stop pressuring your horse *entirely* if you feel the need. Convincing the ambulance driver to use his brakes may be more difficult.

That's why you need to be sure of your preparation. You need to use the skills you've acquired in training when faced with such episodes. However, even in a desperate position, with the ambulance screaming up behind you, you *may* have some options. You can dismount and hold your horse, or you can dart up a side street. Or you can just angle your horse away from the problem and make it through just fine.

Another type of *real-life test* is a formal competitive circumstance, such as a horse show. If you ask your horse to jump a course in competition, you're either able to negotiate it, or not. In a dressage competition, you are expected to perform your transitions (and other movements) at various letters placed at specific points around the arena. You can't circle several times to get your balance right before you execute the movement. You will be judged at how well you can produce the exercise *when asked*. Since competitors can't alter the circumstances if they find their horse over-faced, formal competitions must be treated with as much respect as any other kind of *real-life test*. More harm than good can come if your mount isn't thoroughly prepared.

A *real-life test* will determine whether or not you need to continue training in a more controlled environment, or, if you can continue training at your new, higher, level. Your horse will probably inform you if he's too uncomfortable. When faced with the challenge of confronting city traffic, if your horse merely shudders and continues, finally relaxing, he's telling you that you have judged his readiness and confidence level accurately. Pat yourself on the back.

Testing is necessary in order to push your horse to new levels, but remember, *don't* be impatient, and *don't* attempt more than you or your horse is ready for.

CHAPTER 4

Bombproofing Strategies

In this chapter, I explain various tactics that you can use to compel your horse to obey. Some of these tactics are merely methods of avoiding problems or presenting lessons to your mount in a way that he may find easier to understand. They also encompass a reward and punishment system.

Besides absorbing these general principles, you need *exact strategies* to cope with difficult situations. You need to know what to do when your horse refuses to trek down a path or misbehaves at a parade. Here, I outline the tactics that I've found work best, and use most often.

Diversion

Diverting your horse's attention with another activity is many times the best plan for dealing with problems. A nervous animal will often relax—or at least become more obedient—when asked to focus on a specific task. Here's an example of how you can use everyday work to divert your horse's attention in a stressful situation. Let's say you've taken an inexperienced horse to a place where the atmosphere is highly charged. Maybe you've decided to go on an organized trail ride with a large group of people and horses. Or, maybe you've been blessed with the exciting (and not necessarily pleasant) task of introducing your horse to his first horse show. As part of my responsibilities with the mounted police, sometimes I take unseasoned horses to a parade. So let's say you've ended up in one of these places, with an inexperienced horse.

At a parade, bands might be screeching and trumpeting as they warm up. At a horse show, you might encounter anything from dogs to unruly children who are *clearly* uneducated about green horses. In any of these circumstances, even a group ride, there's bound to be commotion, and lots of it.

As soon as you unload your horse from the trailer, strange sights and sounds overwhelm him. It's hardly a wonder if he begins to quiver. As far as he is concerned, the trailer has landed on another planet, and one that is more than a *little* threatening.

In this type of environment, I immediately get on and ask my mount to perform a task, so that he's more concerned about me, and my demands, than the activity surrounding him. Thus, the animal is given time to acclimate to the mayhem while doing something positive and familiar. These tasks need not be complex to be effective. Getting your horse to focus on *you*—instead of everything else in the world—is the key factor. Almost any type of schooling figures or exercises will help you.

You can work your horse at the trot in a circle or figure eight, asking him to bend in the direction he's going, while insisting that he move forward. You can ask him to perform transitions. You might decide to trot ten strides, walk for three more, and then push him into a canter or a halt, instead. *What* you ask isn't important. What *is* important is that you *vary your requests* so your horse is obliged to listen.

Of course, being a thinking rider, you wouldn't arrive in this type of position without imagining how your horse might react. You always want to stack the odds in your favor. Any situation like this is a *real-life test*, and therefore, requires some pre-planning. You want to make new experiences as easy as possible, for both you and your horse.

You might have brought another horse—a calmer, more experienced one—to assure your horse. You would have checked out the area in advance, to insure that a flat area would be available to work in. And, you wouldn't have brought your horse to begin with if you hadn't remembered to tire him out with a hard workout the day before. In spite of your precautions, since you are in a real-life situation, you'll have limited control over your environment. You may encounter a bunch of bicyclists wheeling past, or even an unruly horse demonstrating all the bad behavior you want to avoid with your mount.

If you're caught in this kind of instance, immediately start practicing an exercise. Pick one. It doesn't matter which. Just do *something* so that your horse's flight response doesn't have time to kick in. Whenever his *comfort zone* has been breached, his instincts will warn him to run. Know it, anticipate it, and stop it before it happens. Managing your horse's flight response is the ultimate in proactive riding. It's also a training tool. If you can control your horse, divert his attention, and ride through his reactions, he learns that what you're asking isn't so impossible after all. While you're working, encourage your horse's willingness with lots of praise and reassurance. When the threat passes, you can congratulate yourself, too, on a difficulty well handled.

Head away is an important exercise in my program (see p. 40). It certainly qualifies as a diversionary tactic, because at its most basic level, it occupies your horse's mind. Your mount is compelled to concentrate on your request, and he has to focus on what his feet are doing, as well. However, I have listed it separately because it's so extraordinarily useful. This is a movement you're going to use a lot—unless you own a saint!

Understand, the number of positive results you get employing *head away* is directly proportional to the time you and your horse have spent practicing it. A green horse won't be as quick to respond to your hand or leg aids. Therefore, the exercise won't be as effective as when performed on a well-schooled animal. The time you spend training is "money in the bank" as far as foiling evasions. When you find yourself holding the reins as a bus roars up behind you, you will find your efforts amply rewarded.

Movement

Letting your horse move, even if only in a circle, is easier than making him stand still, because it allows an outlet for his nerves. Further, movement entails *going forward*, which, so often, is paramount to preventing an evasion. But, sometimes the circumstances dictate that your horse does exactly that—stand still. In a parade, police horses are often put in this awkward situation. Usually, too, it seems like the loudest band is positioned right behind the horses.

When something frightening is behind your animal, his inclination will be to look at it. That way he can tell how close it is and when he needs to start running. To force him to stare ahead when he's convinced the tuba is sneaking up on him may be more than he can bear.

Reassurance

Sometimes merely *letting your horse look* at "the monster" will be enough to reassure him. At least, that way he can make sure a predator isn't about to spring onto his back. In the case of a police horse in a parade, it may look ridiculous to have one horse out of six turned the wrong way, but it is certainly less ridiculous than having your horse flip over backward. This actually happened to one of our officers who refused to let his mount turn out of position. So, to any of my detractors out there who think it undignified of a police horse to turn around in a parade, remember this story. The officer fell off and hit his head, and had to be removed from the parade. How dignified is that?

Of course, sometimes your horse doesn't provide you with the luxury of letting you know his intentions. He may be behaving well, and then abruptly, something will scare him. Anyone acquainted with horses for more than ten minutes has probably experienced a sudden, unpredictable spook. Even the best horse will sometimes do this due to the equine's powerful "prey-animal" instincts.

Have you ever discovered a spider crawling up your arm? Often, before you have time to think about it, your hand will reach up and knock it to the ground. It's the same kind of involuntary response that causes your horse to scoot forward or wheel when he sees or hears a rustle in the bushes. It's ingrained in his genetics to be on the lookout for animals that might eat him, and it's at *least* as difficult for your horse not to react to the noise as it would be for you to not react to the spider.

When you think about the horse's instincts, it becomes obvious that it's almost impossible to train him so he doesn't occasionally react to his environment. And, since you can't prevent the sudden spook from happening, you'll have to ride through it.

First, you have to get your horse back under control. If he bolts, stop him. If he wheels, turn him back in the other direction. In any case, you have to try and stay in the saddle, and at the same time, do something more constructive than freeze in terror. If you sit passively, your horse will make all the decisions. They might not be the best ones, either. Don't forget, the equine has been blessed with a *very* small brain.

After you've corrected your mount's behavior, the most important thing is to *not* make a big production about what happened. *Ignore the "monster."* Your horse will look to you to reinforce or refute his belief that he was justified in being frightened. Sometimes, it can be difficult to keep your cool, because the sheer surprise of a violent spook can often evoke *your* flight or fight response, but remember, even if your heart is racing, *you* have to be the positive role model.

Recently, I was riding a newly acquired draft cross down a street. When we strolled past a trash truck, he decided *something* was going to get him. With no warning, he took off like he was breaking out of the starting gate at a racetrack. To say I was a bit surprised is putting it mildly, but once I got my balance back, I just slowed him to a walk. I didn't make a big deal out of it, and kept moving down the street.

That's a pretty simple example, but the point is that you need to try to stay unemotional and level-headed. Someone once said the ideal trainer has as much temper as a sack of concrete. This doesn't mean you can't punish your horse, only that punishment should be a logical consequence of the horse's actions, not the result of a lack of control over your own feelings.

Direction

Sometimes, just *changing the angle of approach* will convince your horse to do your bidding. I remember a police horse, a strapping, bay gelding with a white face, that resisted walking down a trail near the barn. He would hike all over the property, but, when ridden to the entrance of the trail, he would try to rear. The funny thing was, though, you could ride him *past* the entrance to the trail without problem. He only resisted when you approached it directly.

Tricking him was easier than risking losing a battle with him, so we changed the way we confronted the trail. If you slid in from the side, he had the courage to attempt it. After he was used to going that way, we started approaching from all directions—*including* the direct one. Since he had already experienced success, he was no longer interested in resisting.

There's more than one way to score a touchdown, and a touchdown *is* a touchdown, no matter how it comes about. The same is true of training your horse. Simply because we tricked the bay gelding into forgetting about rearing and instead doing what we wanted, doesn't mean he didn't learn something positive.

Proactive riding, where you prevent an evasion from happening, is a strong training tool. The positive experiences that result will build your horse's confidence, and therefore, his obedience level. Sometimes, walking directly up to a frightening object takes more obedience and courage than your horse can muster. However, in many instances, if you *spiral* around the object instead, gradually getting closer, he will find this an acceptable alternative. The horses in Photos 4.1 to 4.5 began wary of the cage ball, but you'll see, by the end of the session, not only did they actually push the ball around the arena with their noses, but the ball became an actual reward that they sought out and enjoyed.

While you spiral in, you don't need to sit passively. After all, if you simply wait until your horse decides it's okay to get closer, you *could* be there all day. And, why should your mount decide to approach something he thinks might be questionable—even gradually? He's a horse. *You're* the one who wants to walk up to scary things. Therefore, it's *your* job to ask him to breach his *comfort zone*. In this instance, you do this by pushing him closer to the object as you walk, so that he's not entirely relaxed.

This is another occasion where you can use the *headaway* exercise to help you. Remember the mechanics of a spook? Almost always, the horse will want to face the frightening object directly. He'll often start backing-up. The *head away* will place your mount in almost the opposite position. You position his hind end close to the object, and his head farther away, looking the other direction, and as always, you ask him to *go forward*.

Whenever your horse swings away from the object, your leg and hand will be there to produce discomfort. As always, the important thing is to make sure that your horse's actions carry consequences. If he swings his bottom away from the object, you

4.1

4.2

4.3

4.4

4.5

4.1—4.5

Increase Comfort Zone—Spiral to the Cage Ball Obstacle

4.1

The comfort zone between the horses and the cage ball has been established. In order to get closer to the ball, the horses will spiral toward it. The bravest horse should be placed in the lead.

4.2

Working in a spiral, the distance between the horses and the ball is slowly decreasing.

4.3

The horses are closing in on the ball. They are showing interest and seem curious about it. Many times, when a brave horse gets close, other horses will follow the lead.

4.4

The horses have closed in on the ball with one of them actually touching it with his nose.

4.5

The cage ball is pulled away by a ground person while the riders encourage the horses to move toward it. The goal is for the horses to push the ball with their heads or chests.

won't club him over the head, but you *will* make his life less pleasant by definitively using your aids.

As you insist on obedience, working through your mount's reactions, your horse will begin to understand that the object isn't reaching out and trying to grab him. As you repeatedly spiral, he begins to understand that, in fact, the object is just lying there being a hay bale, or bush, or whatever it is. Remember, the repetition is the glue that makes the lesson stick. When you get close enough, you can allow your horse to sniff, touch, and evaluate it. *Sniff, touch, and evaluate,* will be different for each horse; the accompanying pictures show how some horses do it (photos 4.6 to 4.8).

An *angled approach* is valuable for hacking next to something that's long, like a construction site. Simply angle your path, so that as you walk next to the site you get a little closer with each stride. *Leg-yielding* can help to accomplish this. The idea here is the same as spiraling toward something scary, because your horse is asked to confront his fears, but in a graduated way, so he can more easily be successful. Variations of this theme often work for approaching any object. It just requires planning on your part.

However, making the task easier for your horse in no way implies that he doesn't need to comply with your request. Every time he avoids stepping the way you're pushing him, your legs and hands become more active.

Your training, as always, is vital. When mounted on a horse that is disobedient to your aids, or simply lacks the education to understand what they mean, many of the tasks you are trying to accomplish will be impossible, no matter how tactful or clever you are. Develop a solid foundation of training with your flatwork.

I said that almost any exercise can be used to divert your horse's attention, but there *is* one excep-tion. *Backing-up* should only be used sparingly. Remember to use it in limited doses because it can teach the opposite of what you've been trying to ingrain in your horse, which is: *forward, forward, all the time.* He can quickly learn to turn and back-up whenever he is frightened, and further, the rein back positions him in perfect balance to rear—something that must be avoided at all costs.

That being said, there are some instances where you *might* use backing-up to your advantage. When your horse is reluctant to cross something, for exam-ple, you can sometimes back him onto it or through it. For example, if you have a horse that doesn't want to walk in a puddle of water, you can sometimes trick him into entering by backing him into it. This is another sort of proactive riding, and as always, it serves to educate the horse. When your mount finds he is standing in the water, he'll begin to realize his hooves aren't melting off his fetlocks!

Sometimes, though, nothing seems to work. Per-haps you *have* done your homework. You've kept your balance and your temper, and thought ahead. But in spite of all this, and your correctly applied aids, you can't get your horse by the rock, or over the stream, or to do whatever monumental task you've asked him to perform. Even the best rider sometimes can't manage to convince a horse to see things his or her way.

If you truly arrive at a stalemate, then I suggest *working your horse from the ground* discussed in detail in Chapter Five. This is a useful way to resolve a prob-lem when a horse refuses to walk over obstacles while mounted.

4.6—4.8

Sniff, Touch, and Evaluate

4.6

This rider allows her horse to touch and paw the mattress.

4.7

Since this horse spooked at the balloons, the rider allows him to look them over and sniff near them. This helps to calm him down.

4.8

After spooking at the bicycle, this horse is being encouraged to look and sniff. Let your horse investigate items if he shows an interest in doing so.

Hollywood

Competitions can be a fun way to measure the progress that you and your horse have made. Further, besides providing a sort of "report card," they can give you a solid goal to aim for. With these benefits in mind, the police force holds equestrian competitions for officers and their horses.

These events differ from the average horse show because they're designed to test the particular skills needed to be efficient at police work. Competitors typically challenge each other in three categories: the uniform class, the equitation class, and the obstacle class.

The uniform class checks the turnout of officer and mount in infinite detail.

The equitation class judges riders on their positions and effectiveness at the walk, trot, and canter. After narrowing the field, the remaining contestants perform a myriad of tests—the sitting trot, rein back, leg yield, or even hand gallop around the arena. Each judge has favorite tests to help calculate the rider's competence. While the officer's mount is technically not being judged, a well-trained animal is always an asset, and one that misbehaves is almost sure to put you out of the running.

Obstacles courses are my favorite of the three classes, because in my mind, they test the very essence of what the police horse should be—superbly trained for innumerable tasks, brave, steady, and dependable.

The shows themselves vary vastly in size and prestige. They range from the annual, national match, called the Police Equestrian Competition—an event that attracts more than one hundred competitors from all over the United States—to local contests that draw far fewer competitors and are more informal. However, they all provide similar appraisals of the police horse's schooling, obedience, and the officer's skill. It was in one of these local affairs that I competed Hollywood.

Hollywood was a bright bay Thoroughbred with a broad white blaze, and a very decent patrol horse. You could ride him anywhere, from shopping malls to crowd control. He'd tackle obstacles at our training facility with only minor hesitation.

I liked Hollywood and expected him to perform at the police horse competition the way he always did, doing his job without much fuss. It didn't surprise me that he finished well in the equitation class. He stayed on the bit and executed commands reliably.

But the obstacle course was another matter entirely. As soon as we approached the strange ring filled with unfamiliar problems, Hollywood seemed to lose his confidence. I had to boot him with my heels and put him in the *head away* position just to get him in the gate. We managed this supreme feat, but still, his shoulders and flanks shook. It was clear my star mount was quickly deteriorating into a feeble, cowardly shadow of himself.

If the obstacles he was asked to tackle were on the street during a patrol day, he would have easily dealt with each one. However, something about being in a strange ring without any other horses and with all this *stuff* clearly unnerved him. He snorted and sucked closer to the gate. It became obvious that this contest would be a *real-test* situation, and that I would have to use all my talents just to manage him.

The first obstacle was a rectangle, outlined in white. The idea was to stand in it, and then fire a gun, but I couldn't get Hollywood much past the gate. Crops aren't allowed, and he didn't seem to feel my leg at all. None of my tricks worked, not even *head away*. I knew the clock was ticking and we would soon be asked to give up on the first obstacle and attempt the second. So, I used *another* approach. I turned Hollywood around and tried to back into the rectangle. Finally, something effective: it worked.

The judge asked me if I wanted to go ahead and fire the gun, in spite of our difficulties, as a way to get some points. I think he was concerned that Hollywood was going to spook even more, but Hollywood only wanted to leave—and badly! He understood gunfire. He flinched a little while I fired the required two rounds, but stayed right in place, although facing the wrong direction.

Our next task was to traipse up to a car. I was supposed to put a ticket on the windshield. Once again, Hollywood had no interest in leaving the security of the gate. However, this time I knew how to foil him. We backed to the car, and I accomplished my assignment.

I never even turned Hollywood around to see the next obstacle: a guy lying on a bench, covered in a tarp. I just kept backing him. Once next to the man, I turned Hollywood on his haunches, so I could ask the man to get up, as required.

The next test required us to ride between straw bales, over a sheet of plywood that had been covered with bubble wrap. I tried to urge Hollywood forward, but I might as well have been urging a rock. I turned Hollywood around to try backing again, but this time, even *that* didn't work. Finally, we ran out of time and were asked to move to the next challenge.

Now, the bubble wrap obstacle was placed at the far end of the arena, farthest away from the gate. However, the remaining obstacles got progressively closer to the entrance again. Hollywood liked this arrangement much better. He trod over the teeter-totter bridge with barely a glance, since he was aimed in the direction that he wanted to go.

Although he wasn't perfect—he refused the jump the first time he was asked to leap it—he dealt with the remainder of the problems in better and better style, waltzing past the fan blowing streamers, and not flinching at the smoke bomb. His biggest problem was entering that frightening arena all by himself. Except for the bubble wrap, Hollywood wasn't afraid of the obstacles.

Although I was pleased that we had finished with some degree of aplomb, it still wasn't quite the stellar showing I had anticipated. And my peers didn't help. As we slunk from the obstacle course, an officer who knows I do bombproofing clinics hollered out, "Hey, Rick, will you bombproof my horse?"

It's human nature to want our horses to perform well, particularly in a situation like the one I described, where our skills (or lack of them) are on display. However, we, as horsemen, need to remember that since we're riding living creatures instead of machines, there will always be an unpredictable element as to how our horses react to any given circumstance. I thought that we had prepared adequately for the competition, but Hollywood surprised me. Since he performed well both on patrol and in our own arena, it was a reasonable expectation that he would also do so in a strange arena, but that reasonable expectation was dead wrong. Of course, if I decided to compete him again, I realize that it would behoove me to first school him in strange arenas.

At the time, all I could do was use strong riding and management skills to make the best of things. It's impossible to prepare your horse for all possibilities. Therefore, even if you diligently school your mount, you should expect that he nevertheless might need considerable rider support and competence to cope with a situation. Prepare *yourself* accordingly, by developing a strong position and learning management strategies.

CHAPTER 5

Working Your Horse from the Ground

Groundwork, for our purposes, simply means you are going to *lead* your horse over, next to, or through situations.

Please keep in mind, as you read this chapter, that the techniques I'm discussing may require a greater level of horse expertise than you presently possess (see p.17 for an evaluation of your own riding level). If at any time you feel uncomfortable trying these techniques, stop. It may be necessary to find a professional trainer to work through some of the issues. Bombproofing your horse shouldn't be done at your own expense.

If your horse objects to an obstacle, it's sometimes easier, less stressful, and safer to lead him over it first. If you are introducing him to water, he may well resist crossing what he perceives to be dangerous (the hoof-eating water monster). Leading him over it initially avoids you being onboard while he rears,

wheels, or refuses to go forward. It also gets around the problem of trying to stay on him when he *does* decide to tackle the obstacle. He may well jump or bolt over it. If you're unstable in the saddle, he may dump you, leaving you sprawled in the mud.

There isn't any shame in working your horse from the ground to accustom him to new things. The point is to *teach the lesson*. It's not imperative that you're in the saddle to do it. In fact, I often encourage students who are apprehensive about taking a bombproofing clinic to do the entire clinic from the ground.

Tack and Special Equipment for Groundwork
Control Devices
Used for working your horse on the ground, control devices include *chain shanks* and *halters with a moveable nose piece*, which tightens as necessary. A

chain lead shank is the simplest and most available control device. You run the chain through your halter and over your horse's nose.

As I mentioned earlier, I like to use Monty Roberts Dually Halter™ with a "moveable" noseband made of rope (photos 5.1 A to D). See the *Appendix*, page 175, for ordering information. There are similar halters on the market that you may also find suitable. The thinner the rope is, the more severe the device, because the pressure is concentrated in a smaller area.

Using a Chain or Control Halter

The first thing you need to do when using either of these devices is spend a few minutes—literally, that's all—teaching your horse how they work. (This is a separate, different lesson from the one where your horse should follow you over or next to a frightening object.) You want him to understand how he can solve the problem of relieving the discomfort on his nose or head before you throw an additional problem at him. If he has to figure out two problems at once, it may confuse him, take longer, and make the whole operation more painful for both of you.

Start by standing in front of him. Apply a little tension to your lead line. Maintain the tension until he takes a step toward you. As soon as this happens, the pressure on his face will be relieved. It's appropriate for you to reward and praise him at this time.

Your horse should move forward in fairly short order—no more than a few moments. If he appears to be ignoring you, you can increase the pressure on the line in increments. (This shouldn't be difficult since at this point, there's absolutely no reason for him to resist moving forward.)

Repeat this cycle of pulling tension on the line and having your horse "fix the problem" several times, until he understands that *he* is in control of his discomfort, not you. You are his freedom. When he comes forward to you, there is relief and praise. Most horses quickly learn that walking toward you is the correct way to respond.

When he has absorbed this, you can use the same technique to ask him to follow you over something scary. If he really ignores you and just gazes off into the distance, you can "pop" the line once or twice, to remind him to pay attention. However, it is *never* appropriate to use the chain or control halter violently, yanking on it in order to cause the horse pain. Given a little time (usually no more than fifteen minutes), horses will usually choose the path of least resistance and negotiate the obstacle. This is a particularly useful technique for trailer-loading problems.

If your horse panics, throwing his head and neck up and starting to rear, or backing-up rapidly, your best strategy is to *go with him* a bit. Trying to hold him in one place won't work. Further, if he does rear, he may well fall over—either backward or to the side. This is especially true if you keep pulling on him until he finally suddenly breaks free of the pressure on the line. The sudden lack of pressure will often be enough to unbalance him. A thousand-pound-plus animal falling in who-knows-what direction can be dangerous to you, and it isn't a great thing for him, either.

5.1 A—D
Cross Reins and Secure for Groundwork

A. When you plan to use the Dually Halter™ over a bridle, the reins need to be safely secured. Start with the reins over the neck, bring them close to the ears, take up the slack, and make a circle by crossing the near rein (left side) over the far rein (right side).

B. Pass the "circle" of reins over the horse's head.

C. The crossed reins rest on the horse's neck—out of the way.

D. With the reins out of the way, place the Dually Halter™ over the bridle. A longe or lead line may be attached to the loose ring. When the horse pulls away, the moveable nose piece tightens, and when the horse stops pulling, it loosens.

Safety Considerations

Keep a safe distance. The first thing to remember is to keep a safe distance from your horse. This means keeping as far away as possible. When using your bridle reins to lead him, you'll only be able to stay an arm's length away. Keep one hand on him if you are at this distance. This way you can feel his intentions and react accordingly. If he creeps closer, simply cock your arm so your elbow pokes into him. This alone will often keep him at a safe distance.

A long lead line or longe line will allow you to create more distance between you and your horse. Furthermore, you can swap the side you're leading him from, when needed. The more options you have, the easier your task will be, and you'll be safer, as well.

Don't get tangled in the lead line. The longer the line, the more skill you need in keeping the line organized. If it dangles on the ground, it can become knotted. Your horse can step on it or through it, causing considerable panic on his part. It can also get wrapped around your feet, which is potentially deadly.

Don't wrap any line around any body part. A loop of rope—even if it's loose—can quickly be pulled tight around your hand. You run the risk of losing fingers or being dragged.

Don't get trampled. Most of the other safety considerations I discuss here are simply ways to avoid being trampled. Leading a horse over or past something scary often initiates his flight response. He may suddenly rush forward, backward, or even sideways. If you are too close—or just standing in the wrong spot—he may bump into you, trip you, run over you, or step on you.

Watch what your horse's body language tells you. Remember you are habituating your horse to something scary. Look at him! Now is not the time to sightsee or daydream. Watch his eyes, body, and feet. His eyes and ears tell you what he is concerned with and the amount of fear or obstinacy you are facing. If you are in front of him, look at his chest. Watching his "center" is a more reliable way to guess which way he'll go than watching his legs. These indicators will all help you to predict what his next move will be.

Expect him to shy away from the obstacle. If you're leading your horse past a scary object, expect him to shy away from it. *Stay on the same side as the scary thing*, because otherwise, your mount will shy into *you*. The accompanying photos 5. 2 A & B show Baldwin, a six-year-old Connemara/Arab, shying away from the obstacle and moving away from his handler, Mary Ellen. He didn't run into her because she was positioned safely. The photos also show her working from both sides of the horse.

It helps to become ambidextrous. Most of us are conditioned to always do everything from the horse's near (left) side. Because of this, we often feel uncomfortable leading our horses from the off side. However, if you spend a few minutes thinking about it and then doing it, this new skill will become easy. Be smart, anticipate the problem, and place yourself on the same side as the object. Then, when he shies, he'll move safely away from, and not into, you.

Learn to walk backward. As you encourage your horse to follow you over an obstacle, face him at all times. It's impossible for you to prepare for your horse's reaction if your back is to him. This will often mean you need to walk backward. I have seen more than one person get bowled over when her horse suddenly lurched forward over an obstacle. Inevitably, she was facing forward and not watching her horse.

Anticipate him jumping or running toward you. When your horse follows you over something scary—a tarp, a creek, a funny-looking log—he may suddenly leap forward and jump the obstacle. This is when maintaining your distance becomes so vital. Nevertheless, your horse can quickly close this distance when he jumps or runs toward you.

Often, your mount will want to come right to you for security. In fact, he will often want to be standing in the *exact* spot that you occupy—an uncomfortable proposition. In this instance, you can increase your safety and exert control over his response by doing what I call "throwing up a wall." Lifting your hands up toward his face will usually slow or even stop him. This motion establishes a barrier between you.

Step to the side. This is easier and quicker than trying to run backward.

5.2 A & B
Leading by Obstacles

Place yourself between the obstacle and the horse so that if he is afraid and tries to escape, he will move away from, and not into, you. When training, always lead from both left and right sides of the horse.

Ground School with or without Tack?

You may or may not have tack on your horse for ground schooling. When dealing with a green horse, or an extremely nervous horse, you may elect to leave your mount untacked for several sessions. In a situation where you have reached an impasse with a normally compliant horse, you might dismount and use existing tack, or simply grab a halter and lead rope.

With Tack

1 If you have an English saddle, run the irons up, or flip them over the saddle (photos 5.3 A & B). Those metal stirrups hurt when they start flying around! This is not an issue with Western saddles.

2 Realize that you have limitations using your bridle and its reins to lead your horse. Bridles, of course, are designed for riding. The first problem is that they don't really give the horse much incentive to move forward (like a control halter might) when you are on the ground. Second, the reins limit the distance you can create between you and your horse, so you run an increased risk of being trampled. Finally, the length of the reins also makes it hard to hold onto your horse if he misbehaves. If you drop the reins, your horse might step on them. He can get tangled or simply break them.

In a pinch, you can double the length of rein you have to work with by unfastening the rein on one side by the bit. On some bridles, this is a very simple procedure but with others, it is impractical.

Sometimes, however, a bridle does work, especially if the horse will accompany the rider quietly. If the horse backs-up, rears, or performs any kind of negative behavior, a bridle won't be effective.

5.3 A & B
Running the Stirrups Up

A. *Whenever dismounted, always run the stirrups up to keep them from swinging and hitting you.*

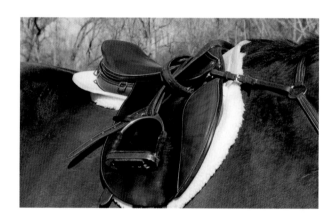

B. *Another way to get stirrups out of the way is to cross them over the saddle.*

3 If you put a halter on over a bridle, make sure it clears the bit and sits up over the nose. Secure the reins either under the throatlatch or by doubling them around the neck.

Without Tack

1 Use a halter (see *Control Devices*, p. 77) and lead rope or longe line. The longer the lead, the better, so the handler can keep a safe distance and still maintain effective control.

2 Make sure the halter fits. If it is not put on snugly, it can get pulled to the side and into your horse's eye when you apply pressure.

Additional Items

A long whip, like a longe whip, can be employed from behind to help drive a resistant animal over an obstacle. If the whip is too short, the person using it will have to stand too close to his rear end and run the risk of being kicked. *Gloves* are vital when using a nylon lead rope or longe line. If your horse pulls, the line can instantly, and severely, burn your hands.

A head bumper is a good idea when working a horse with a loading problem. Tall horses are particularly prone to bash themselves in the poll, but more than occasionally, even the shorter varieties will throw up their heads as they exit the trailer. Utilizing a head bumper as a safety precaution eliminates vet bills, stitches, and negative habituation. If your horse injures himself loading, he may well conclude it was the trailer that "bit" him, and become even more hesitant about going into it.

The General Plan

Your goal is to get your horse used to a scary object—to habituate him to it. You may want him to step over it, through it, or just walk by it. When working from the ground, you follow the same format you follow in all of your bombproofing endeavors.

1. Minimize the Obstacle

This just means making it easy. If you're trying to habituate him to something man-made in a controlled environment, minimizing an obstacle is, of course, simpler than trying to accomplish the same thing out on the trail. You can always fold up a tarp or make a jump into a rail on the ground. It's not so simple with a stream.

However, the obstacle must not be too daunting at first. If you're accustoming your horse to a stream, you will simply have to find one that is reasonably inviting (this means finding one with a flat, shallow approach, and decent footing). If you're trying to get him closer to an obstacle, as opposed to over it, you can make it less challenging by initially allowing him to walk by it at a distance.

Somehow, you need to figure out a way to make the task less testing. In Chapter Seven, *Bombproofing Day*, I explain exactly how to minimize a whole slew of obstacles. However, the list of things your horse may find frightening is endless, so you'll have to use your imagination if you don't find it on *my* list!

2. Attempt the Obstacle

This may be easy, or you may need to use one or more of the following methods:

Make him follow you.
Sometimes just the idea that *you're* going to cross the scary obstacle first will be enough to convince your horse to follow—but of course, not always.

Make him follow another horse.
Use your horse's herding instinct to your advantage, and have an experienced horse go first.

Keep him moving forward.
This can often do the trick. It's important because he needs to stop his forward motion in order to perform an evasive maneuver.

Make him cross his legs.

If he locks his legs and refuses to move, you can get him going again by just pulling his head to one side so his legs are forced to cross. Once he is in motion, he will frequently be inclined to stay in motion. This can be a surprisingly effective strategy. The horses in the accompanying photographs absolutely refused to budge—they were completely "locked." However, by turning their heads and unbalancing them, it was eventually possible to cross the obstacle (See photos 5.4 A & B and 5.5 A—D).

Have someone get behind him with a whip.

This is another way to encourage him forward. It's a two-person operation, with one leading the horse, and the other wielding the whip. Many times, just seeing a whip being held behind him will be enough incentive to convince him to obey. However, if that isn't enough, you can tap your horse on his hind end and gauge his response. Increase the pressure in increments, allowing him the opportunity to respond to as little force as possible. If you rush in and "attack" him, you may do nothing more than cause panic on his part. You want the situation to remain calm and controlled.

The person employing the whip needs to stand a safe distance from the horse's backside. If she threatens him with a whip, she may become a prime target for a kick.

3. Perform Repetitions

One trip through the water or over a tarp won't teach him much. You need to repeat the exercise until your horse demonstrates that he's no longer concerned (he shows this by negotiating the obstacle calmly several times). It may take him three times, or thirty, to relax. When you're successful, you can either call it a day or up the challenge.

I should add that while one bombproofing session may be enough to accustom your horse to the new obstacle, it isn't always the case. Some horses need the lesson repeated on subsequent days before it really sinks in.

4. Make the Obstacle Harder

If your horse isn't too frazzled (or you aren't), you can slowly increase the difficulty of what you're asking him, and repeat the steps above. However, you should remember that you always want to end on a good note. Use discretion.

5. Transition to Riding the Obstacle

Obviously, you eventually want to ride your horse through the situation. After all, if you just want to walk an animal on a leash, you can get a dog. Once he is at ease and tackling the obstacle confidently, mount up.

When you try to ride him over the obstacle, your horse may still have some misgivings, even if he has become totally accustomed to it while being led. It's different when he has to attempt it by *himself!*

If you have a friend to assist you, she can lead the horse over several times with you onboard. Then, she can simply walk in front of you as if he is still "hooked up" on a line. As your horse gets more comfortable, she can leave the picture entirely.

In an uncontrolled environment, or if you don't have assistance, you'll have to use your active riding skills to convince him to comply. After your horse attempts the obstacle while mounted, you'll need to perform repetitions again, until he is relaxed and confident.

5.4 A & B
Horse "Locking Up" at the Mat

Here, the horse has "locked up" at the mat obstacle. I lead him to one side to "unlock" his legs and ask him to move forward again. Once his legs are unlocked, I'll ask him, once again, to cross the mat. Note that I'm keeping a safe distance so that if, like many horses, he decides to jump the obstacle, he doesn't run into me.

5.5 A—D
Here is another horse "locked up" at the mat obstacle. Once again, he was led to one side to get his legs to cross. As soon as he moved to the side, I asked him to move toward me and cross the mat, which he did in both directions.

CHAPTER 6

Dealing with Bad Habits and Nasty Tricks

In this chapter, I am going to discuss corrections and preventive measures for the most common types of behavior problems, in this order: *rearing; bucking; backing-up; whirling and spinning; shying; spooking in place; locking up; herd bound; refusal to stand quietly; not standing still during mounting;* and *bolting.* I deal with each of these issues individually, but before proceeding, you need to ask yourself three questions:

Step 1
Can I deal with my horse's bad behavior?
If you're wondering how you decide when you might be able to fix a problem, and when you should just phone a professional, the answer depends on the training level and personality of your horse, and the

level of your own skill. I find quite often at my clinics that I'm successful at advancing a horse, while his rider is not. Every situation, and every horse-and-rider combination, are different, and a less experienced rider can exacerbate a dangerous behavior problem.

Why? Remember the three T's (p. 29). The rider's *technique* is wrong, she doesn't perform the *training* exercises correctly, or she does the exercise at the wrong *time*. It's largely a matter of experience and skill. Reading how to fix a problem in a book is simpler than actually fixing the problem. It is extremely perilous for the casual rider to try to re-school an animal with a serious, reoccurring behavior problem.

Step 2
Is it a bad habit or just a bad day?

You need to differentiate between the animal that possesses well-established evasive behavior and the animal that only exhibits his adverse behavior when extremely stressed. I remember riding a gelding that had never reared—until the day we did an exhibition with a smoke bomb. The officer on the ground lit the bomb too close to the gelding's feet. Clearly shocked, the gelding stood straight up on his hind legs. This wasn't due to a flaw in his training, and it wasn't a bad habit. It was simply an indication that the animal was surprised by what was going on. He never did it again.

If your horse behaves badly only when you ask him to perform an especially terrifying task—like standing still while some fool lights a smoke bomb next to him—this is certainly a different (and better) problem to deal with than the one presented by the beast that has learned to use rearing as a sure-fire way to avoid *anything* that resembles work.

If your horse unveils his troubling behavior only under stressful conditions, and only occasionally, you'll probably be all right. *Most* horses will try to avoid situations they're worried about. Nevertheless, you need to carefully scrutinize your own skills and feelings about dealing with occasional bad behavior. You can be hurt even if your mount only occasionally acts up. Further, if anticipation and worry are spoiling your enjoyment of riding, you should consider buying a more suitable horse as a partner. (See p. 7 for guidance.)

But let's say your horse does not intimidate you, and he only wheels around when he has to traipse by particularly frightening rocks. You need to know how to best deal with the evasion. What follows are corrections and preventive measures you can use for the more common types of behavior problems.

Step 3
Do I understand my horse's problem so I can figure out the proper corrective and preventive measures?

Rearing
The Problem

Rearing is the ultimate refusal to move forward. The most serious consequence of it is the potential of the horse toppling over—and landing on you. This danger is accentuated by the rider's perfectly natural tendency to hang on to the reins for support, which may well pull the animal off balance enough to result in a fall.

The Solution

Your horse has launched himself in the air. When his front hooves have left the ground, his forelock is in your eyes, and your heart has sprinted up your throat—what do you do?

The rule here is to *survive*. When a horse successfully rears, *he* is in control. Until all four feet are back on the ground, the most that you can do is try to stay on board and avoid being injured. Even if you're taken totally by surprise, you still need to resist the temptation of hauling on the reins. The correct response is to throw your weight and hands toward his ears. Grab some mane if you need to hold on to something. I generally ride with a breastplate and subsequently, have that to clasp onto in an emergency.

Horses that have learned to rear as an evasion are usually very good at it and know their balance point well. A green horse that spontaneously soars skyward is more dangerous because he's not as balanced. Consequently, the rider can easily affect his stability.

Once the horse is back on the ground, you need

to react immediately to correct him, which I'll discuss in a moment. But first, let's reverse a step, and think about how to *prevent* your horse from rearing in the first place, which of course, is the best-case scenario. If you know your horse is inclined to rear, you probably already know when it is coming, or at least when he is thinking about it.

What are the warning signs that a rear might be imminent? Think about how this section began. *Rearing is the ultimate refusal to go forward.* When you ride—in any gait, even at the walk—your horse should give you the feeling he has a destination and he's bound to arrive. Instead, when considering rearing, he will tend to make hesitant, halting motions. He raises his head and neck. He may move erratically, careening from side-to-side. His front end will become "lighter," as he shifts more weight onto his hind legs. These are all potential preparations for rearing.

If you feel these warning signals, attempt to drive your animal forward. An increase in pace will make it more difficult for him to rear. Think of it this way. Could a galloping horse rear? Even if he tried, it would end up being a jump. The horse actually has to *stop* his forward movement in order to rear successfully.

But what if driving your mount forward more aggressively doesn't work? Maybe the second your horse feels the spurs tickling his sides, his response isn't to dash ahead, but merely to begin resisting in earnest. This isn't that unusual. You may have to adjust your tactics—but the idea is the same.

Generally, the horse resists moving forward and rears because he doesn't want to negotiate an obstacle in front of him. So, at the moment you ask him to move forward, redirect him into a circle. Either direction will do. Remember, the horse is still moving forward—only on a circle, instead of a straight line.

You may think that your horse got away with avoiding the obstacle in front of him, but there is a bigger, more important picture here—*obedience to your driving aids.* Your horse must respond to a request to go forward with an increase in pace, even if it's not in exactly the direction you had originally planned. You are reinforcing the idea that rearing is not an option.

As you circle, you need to remember to *push.* When your animal does move willingly forward on the circle at the increased pace, drive him straight ahead again. Each time you feel he's preparing to rear again, repeat the exercise, immediately circling.

The exercise won't work unless you remind your animal to respond to the leg positively—that is, with an increase in pace—while you circle. Gradually, you should progress closer to the rock or stump or puddle that your horse has decided is monstrous. Essentially, your horse is forced to respond to the driving aids by going forward. At some point, the animal will decide that it's easier to go where you wish than be circled and kicked. However, you may have missed the warnings your horse sent you. Perhaps you were contemplating the serenity of the forest while your mount was contemplating dumping you in the leaves.

If your horse has already successfully reared, remember the advice for riding it out at the beginning of this section. Provided you're still in one piece when he's arrived back down on all fours, you need to punish him for his actions. No, not by beating him—but he *does* need to understand that there are consequences for his actions. You're going to use much the same strategy to correct his behavior as you would to prevent it.

When you've landed, immediately direct him into a tight circle, asking him to move forward at a trot. Remind him with your leg that moving forward, *not* upward, is the correct response to your pushing aids. After several circles, push him straight again. Be prepared for your horse to attempt his bad behavior again, and try and prevent it. He might not be easily convinced that the best course of action is to obey you. This is particularly true if he's successfully been avoiding work he dislikes for a long time with *his* strategy. Remember to praise him lavishly for responding positively.

However, encourage and praise *only* when your mount responds positively. Too many times I've witnessed a rider patting her horse immediately after he rears. I suppose she thinks she is calming her horse, or maybe she's just trying to negotiate, but it doesn't work that way. Praising bad behavior only encourages it.

Use one consistent word, in one consistent tone, when correcting your mount's behavior. I simply say "quit" when the horse is doing something wrong. He will begin to understand the word means he is misbehaving if it is backed up with consequences. Although your horse can learn the meaning of a word—or at least the meaning of the tone associated with it—he will never grasp complex sentences. It may please *you* to explain to your horse that the water won't hurt him, but don't expect it to affect *his* actions much.

But what if you're attempting to stand in one spot when your horse rears? Your strategy will have to change a bit. Sometimes when our officers are training horses to stand on line (to confront demonstrators in crowd control), we have to deal with this problem. To add to the dilemma, many horses that normally never consider rearing may do so under enough pressure, and crowd control can undeniably be stressful.

Even in a situation where movement is limited, the mechanics are the same. The horse has to shift his weight to his hind legs to rear successfully.

A *turn on the forehand* can work wonders in this instance, because the horse's hind legs cross as they move around his forehand. This makes it difficult for him to change his weight to his backside.

Bucking
The Problem
When your horse bucks, he weights his forehand to the extent that his hind legs come off the ground—the opposite of what happens when he rears. Although a "balky" horse may kick or even buck when protesting the use of leg or spur, many times a buck isn't malicious. Sometimes, it's just the physical expression of excitement or of an inability to deal with pressure. Bucking normally isn't as unsafe as rearing, simply because the rider doesn't run the risk of being squashed. However, it can certainly result in a fall (of the rider), which *can* be dangerous and is *never* fun.

The Solution
Though the way the horse uses his body is different, bucking (like rearing) can be interrupted and *minimized* by keeping your horse going forward. You may have watched broncos in the rodeo cover ground as they buck, but in reality, they still need to hesitate every time they whip their rear ends toward the sky. It isn't possible for them to buck as *efficiently* when moving ahead. Your horse also needs to lower his head and neck in preparation for a good, hard, rider-blasting buck. He uses them to counter-balance his hind end.

Your horse may warn you he intends to blow-up with indicators peculiar to him—such as his hindquarters bouncing from side-to-side—or his behavior may be difficult to predict. In any event, when you feel your horse's back come up and his head suddenly plunge, you need to simultaneously pull his head up and drive him forward. Obviously, a deep seat and dropped heels are assets in this situation.

Backing-Up
The Problem
Sometimes your horse may back-up away from a situation to avoid it.

The Solution
Always try to first correct the problem by urging him forward. If even the whip or spurs don't do the trick, you should immediately displace your horse's hind end with a *turn on the forehand*. Once your horse's hind end is displaced, it will be impossible for him to continue backing.

Try turning your mount's head either way. Often, this simple strategy will produce positive results, though it's not as dynamically effective as having the hind legs cross.

Whirling or Spinning
The Problem
If your horse is inclined to whirl or spin, the good news is that he will nearly always whip around in the same direction. In fact, the only reason that I say "nearly" is that horses tend to make liars of those foolish enough to say "always." However, every case of whirling that I've dealt with has reinforced my belief that as far as this form of resistance is concerned, horses are creatures of habit.

The Solution
Let's imagine you're riding along peacefully when your horse spots something *he* imagines is frightening. He whirls to the left in an attempt to flee.

Your correction will be to turn him back to the right (the *opposite* direction of his spin). Remember to drive him forward with your leg. You'll make sev-

eral circles to the right, until you feel your horse willingly move ahead. Of course, some horses easily figure out how to outwit this strategy. Sometimes, the horse braces on the rein (in this case, it would be the right one) and rears. Now you have a double problem.

But rearing is the dilemma that takes precedence. Since rearing is the habit, above all others, that you don't want to encourage, you should immediately turn the horse back to the left (the way he is *inclined* to spin). Circle him several times to the left, while you demand he move forward. Does circling the way your horse desires imply he is getting his way? *No.* You are in control, making him circle. You have chosen the lesser of two evils, but, in both cases, *there are consequences for his actions*.

Of course, prevention is even better than fixing a problem. How do you avoid this whole mess and thwart whirling before it begins?

Let's start over, imagining the same scenario as above—your peaceful ride is interrupted when your horse's body language alerts you that he's spotted a worrisome object. As usual, this can be anything: a herd of cows, an oddly colored rock, or a bush being whipped around by the wind. But, it's of little consequence that a fluttering bush is about as dangerous as, well... a fluttering bush.

Your mount is afraid nonetheless. His ears are pricked, and his heart races like he's just galloped a mile. He's raised his head so high you can barely peek over his poll, and his muscles are clenched tight. He's done everything but send you a telegraph to warn you he's about to spin.

Since you already know which direction he'll choose, you can avert the problem. We'll say *left* is your horse's favorite direction. *Immediately*, ask your horse for a *right head away*. The aids for *right head away* are similar to the aids for circling to the right—

the correction you'd use if he managed to whirl. This exercise encourages the horse to give to the bit, and bends him away from the direction he's thinking of wheeling.

What you've accomplished is turning off the soup before it's boiled over. You've reminded your equine to be obedient to the leg and hand *before* he's disobeyed. Giving to the bit and lowering his head help him to concentrate on your wishes; and further, a lowered head will assist in relaxing him.

Shying
The Problem
Shying hardly needs to be explained to anyone who rides. But it's sure not fun.

The Solution
Shying can be prevented in a similar fashion as whirling. When something to the side scares your horse, he'll attempt to face the object while simultaneously moving away from it. When his head swings one way, his bottom will swing the opposite way—*away* from the object of fear. The problem is that your horse's instincts aren't always intertwined with logic. While your horse's *front end* is busy confronting a particularly dangerous looking rock, a car may sideswipe his back end.

To prevent shying, as with any evasion, you have to be able to anticipate it. If you've been partners with your horse for some time, you probably have more than an inkling of what might disturb him. But even if you haven't, your horse may well give you clues. Sidling away from an object, a hesitant gait, or just scrutinizing something a bit too intently are signals that you need to act before he does.

To counter a problem on your *right* side, put your horse into a *left head away*. This accomplishes several things. First, the *left head away* bends your

horse's head slightly left, away from the "monster," so he won't be able to look at it. When your horse isn't directly facing the problem, he sees a way out of the situation. He'll actually gain confidence from your request. Further, focusing on crossing his legs and listening to your request will help to refocus your mount's energy in a more positive manner.

When your horse suddenly shies, it's more a matter of damage control. You have to react quickly. If your horse leaps sideways unexpectedly and jumps to the left, your correction would be to use left rein and left leg pressure. I know it may sound confusing to use the aids suggested, but you're *not* turning your horse left. Your horse is shying by looking to the right and spinning his hind end to the left. Your left rein counters his action and straightens his face. Your simultaneous left leg pressure will straighten his hind end.

This is another instance where the time you've invested in learning flatwork will benefit you. To use your aids in the correct combination to obtain the desired result takes a bit of practice. It can feel awkward to push your horse sideways at first, sort of like scratching your head and rubbing your stomach at the same time. Do your homework.

Spooking in Place
The Problem
When a horse is suddenly frightened and drops down like an elevator, I call it "spooking in place." Most of you have felt this reaction aboard a horse at some point—where your horse's knees buckle, his hocks bend, and he suddenly shrinks six inches. Though the horse doesn't really go anywhere, sometimes he ducks to one side.

The Solution
Unfortunately, the only solution I have for this is to

simply ride it out. You may not think that's much of a suggestion, but remember, this happens suddenly and unexpectedly. Since you can't *anticipate* it, you can't *prevent* it.

However, your reaction to your horse in this situation is still important. It's your job to instill confidence, to assure him that everything is okay. As I've stressed before, *you're* the leader of your little herd. Your horse will take his cues from you. You have to develop a composed mind-set. Panic, on your part, will only convince your animal that *his* fear is justified.

I know your adrenaline is flowing, but, after your horse has finished spooking, you need to continue your ride as if nothing had happened. In fact, this applies to all of the situations described here as well. Once a bad situation has passed, it's finished. Force a smile on your face. You may feel like beating your horse, but it wouldn't help if you did. Try to think in terms of *correcting* your horse's behavior, instead of punishing him for it. Don't overreact.

Of course, your security in the saddle is at least as important as your attitude. When your horse spooks and drops down, you *must* stay loose and go with him. Many times the rider will become tense and go into what some horsemen laughingly refer to as "the fetal position." However, the humorous term accurately describes what tension can do to your seat. This position, marked by raised heels, hunched back, and curled-over posture, may be the best one for an unborn child, but is not suitable for a rider.

The fetal position forces your weight forward and increases your risk of falling. Attempt to sit tall, straight and deep. Try to get in the habit of grabbing the mane, pommel, or the strap of your breastplate in an emergency (a good investment if your mount is inclined toward this kind of behavior). A handful of leather can help you stay balanced in the saddle.

Being quick and instinctive are always assets, but are ones that come with experience.

Locking Up
The Problem
Locking up, or refusing to move, is the term for what happens when your horse grows so tense that he becomes completely immobile. Usually, he will seem immune to the pressure of your spurs, or even the slap of your whip. Eventually, though, he *will* do something. The problem is, you don't know what that *something* will be. When you've finally convinced him that permanent paralysis isn't a good solution to dealing with stress, watch out! He may rear, bolt, or back-up uncontrollably.

The Solution
The first thing you need to do is unlock your horse's legs. A *turn on the forehand* is often effective (p. 39.) Your practice and training in lateral movements will once again reward you. You'll be confident in how to use your aids, and it will be second nature for your horse to respond to them.

If I haven't convinced you to read about (much less *practice*) flatwork, you can still effectively shift your horse's weight so he's forced to move. Pick up contact with your reins, but not so much that you encourage backing-up. Remember, *forward* movement is nearly always your friend in overcoming resistance—and backing-up is its *opposite*.

Next, choose either rein, lift it, and bring it slightly across the withers. Simultaneously apply leg pressure behind the girth on that same side (in other words, use the left rein and leg together, or the right rein and leg together). Using the *right* rein and leg will result in his hind end moving *left*. The correct amount of pressure is the amount that gets the result.

Of course, the quality of the movement isn't what counts in this situation. All you're attempting to do is unlock your beast's hind end and get him going. Once he *is* unlocked—the absolute *moment* his paralysis fades—try to get him moving forward in a circle. The idea is to avoid his *next* maneuver, which could be that bolting, rearing, or backing-up trick.

Still doesn't work? Another option is to move your horse's front end laterally, with a *turn on the haunches* (p. 40). Open one of your reins. Let's say you choose the *right* one. "Opening" means to move the rein away from your horse's neck, like you were hitchhiking with that hand. At the same instance, use your left rein against his neck as you carry your hand to the right. *Both* of your reins have now moved to the right.

At the same time, you need to push with your legs. Your right calf will press behind your horse's girth, while your left leg presses into his left shoulder. Applied simultaneously, these aids should be enough to get your horse to shift to the right, and possibly cross his legs as well. As your mount unlocks and moves his front end laterally, his hind end will follow around the circle.

This strategy also applies to situations when you're working your horse in hand (from the ground). If he decides to stop and refuses to walk forward, pulling doesn't usually work. You can haul on him, but he's liable to stay rooted to the spot, head braced against you like a donkey. Sometimes, he'll even back away.

The solution to this problem is to immediately take up the slack in the lead line or reins, and step to the side. When you tug his head to the side, it will force him to step laterally. It's physically impossible for him to refuse to move. If you combine this scheme with the use of a restraint over his nose, it's doubly effective. Re-read Chapter Five, *Make Him*

Cross His Legs, for more information on this training technique (p. 84).

Herd Bound
The Problem
Managing a horse that is herd bound can be challenging, because you're fighting Mother Nature. *Most* horses want to be close to their equine buddies. Strong instincts warn your mount that his safety may well depend on his ability to keep up with the herd. These instincts can be valuable training tools when manipulated to your needs, but they can also be obstacles.

Wanting to leave the group (or even worse, the group leaving *you*), will tend to bring out the worst behavior in your animal. Some horses possess the added trait of being competitive, which can reveal different sorts of problems. Falling in *this* category is the horse that has to be in front on a trail ride. However, in either instance, the way I wean the horse from his buddies is the same.

The Solution
Before you begin, you need to garner some help from other riders. Without their absolute cooperation, this exercise will be impossible.

This lesson—like all others you attempt to teach your horse—starts simply, in a confidence-building format. As your equine masters the easier steps, you can progress to the more difficult ones. Don't expect to resolve this issue in one lesson, or even in several. It will take time, and many repetitions.

To start, turn away, going off to one side, or reverse direction. Make sure that *you* leave the group at first—far easier than having them leave you. Move off at a trot (remember, going forward is your friend) while the group stays at a walk or halt. At first, a short distance will do.

While still within sight of the others, return to the group at a walk. Only walk! Your horse's instincts will be screaming at him to rush back to the crowd before he is attacked by a cougar, so you may have to reinforce your request to go slowly. If he tries to trot or canter back, immediately change direction again, away from the group. Eventually, he'll understand that hurrying only leads to being asked to depart again. Repeat the exercise.

How many times? The answer is always the same—whatever it takes. When he seems comfortable, or at least his behavior improves, you have two choices. You can press your horse further, by making the exercise more difficult, or you can quit. If your mount is obviously stressed and it has taken a hour to master jogging half a block away from his friends, the smart choice would be to go home.

You have to muster the fortitude to ride out and manage your horse's fears while doing this. You also have to be more determined than he is. Be patient. *Expect* your horse to react, to holler for the other horses, for them to answer. *Expect* your horse to sweat, prance, and toss his head. *Try* not to let it bother you. We all know this kind of behavior can be extremely annoying, but remember the best trainer has the temperament of a sack of potatoes, that is, he's not given to temper or fear, or even bursts of wild praise.

To break through to an improved level, understand that you're breaching your horse's *comfort zone.* You have to ride out the rough spots. It should help your confidence to realize you can teach your mount in very small bites, if that's what makes you secure. You're the one in charge.

While the easiest form of this exercise is simply to hack a short distance from the group, keeping them in sight, the next step is to hack a bit further, *out* of sight. Finally, you can begin to experiment with the other riders leaving *you.* The most difficult form of this exercise is to have your horse wait while his buddies thunder off at a gallop.

Refusal to Stand Quietly
The Problem
Many horses refuse to stand quietly. Frequently, otherwise good horses lack this simple, most basic of skills. I can only speculate that most people rush to the barn before or after work, hop on their horse, and *go.* Whether the rider is constrained by a limited time frame, or focused on developing the animal for a specific sport (therefore using most of their moments riding either training or performing), many times, this bit of schooling is ignored.

Teaching this skill is a recurrent situation for me, because a police horse *must* possess it. Oftentimes, he is asked to stand for long periods, and sometimes in uncomfortable conditions.

The Solution
For you to teach your mount, you have to change his routine. Although you *can't* force him to hold still, you *can* offer alternatives. When he starts to fidget, put him to work. Ride him in a circle or a figure-eight pattern. Other options are performing a turn on the forehand or the haunches. Whatever you choose, though, always finish the movement by returning to the same spot. The point? You'll have distracted him by making him work, and he's still ended up in the same location.

You have to be more persistent than your horse, and we all know a horse can be a very determined creature, indeed. However, if you give up, you'll never improve him. Anticipate that the training process will take time, and allow for it. You should devote at least a half-hour to this lesson, and expect to repeat it *at least* several times before it "sticks."

The last horse I trained with this method took several days to absorb it. While on patrol with him I repeated it, at intervals. Of course, I didn't do this for six hours a day, I'm simply illustrating that you won't fix this in one ten-minute session. Your horse should ultimately stand indefinitely. If you have an extremely determined horse, I would suggest that you dismount and stand with him. If he fidgets, walk him in a circle, returning to the same spot. Once he improves, try the mounted exercises again.

Not Standing Still During Mounting
The Problem

Not only annoying, this habit is potentially dangerous. Maybe you're used to it, but throwing a leg over your horse's back while he's moving is *not* safe.

The Solution

To correct this behavior, position your horse so his head faces a wall or fence. That way, he can't walk forward. I also use a mounting block initially, because it allows me to concentrate on my rein control.

Before you attempt to mount, gather your reins so you have contact with your horse's mouth and are able to stop any forward movement. Put your foot in the stirrup, but hesitate momentarily before throwing your leg over his back. This is the critical time to make a correction with your reins if he attempts to move forward. Don't throw your leg over until he's still. Your foot will stay in the stirrup as long as your horse is quiet. If your horse starts to act up and moves, slip your foot out of the stirrup. That way, you won't get hurt. Reorganize your horse and start again. If he sidles away, use a corner of the fence to block his movement. If he backs-up? Then, you'll need an assistant on the ground to reinforce your request for him to stand quietly. Have your assistant stand on the near (left) side of your horse,

holding the cheek piece of the bridle, but not the reins, because *you'll* require them.

Your horse may push to the right, the left, into your assistant, or into you. Try to anticipate these problems. In any event, you should only attempt to mount while your horse is standing still. Between the fence and your assistant, you should be able to thwart your horse's movement. If your horse simply *can't* stand still, call in a full-time professional for help.

Once your horse has mastered this, you can repeat the exercise in an open area. Now you *will* need an assistant, even if your horse learned the first part of this exercise with only the fence to help steady him. Remember, don't throw your leg over until he stands still. If your saddle is slipping, you need another person to press down on the opposite stirrup with his hand.

Repeat this until you can mount without your assistant. Then, lose the mounting block. Like any of the other problems, this one may take more than a single lesson to fix. Don't hesitate to backtrack and use your assistant again if you start having problems.

Bolting
The Problem

If your horse runs uncontrollably when frightened, you have a serious safety problem. A bolting horse may well leap into traffic or land you in other dangerous circumstances. You need to consider what riding an animal like this may possibly cost you.

The Solution

If you do find yourself on a runaway, you need to try and find a way to redirect his energy. Try to turn him in as tight a circle as possible to make it more difficult for him to run. Sometimes, the horse is so frightened that he doesn't respond to your

6.1 A & B
The Pulley Rein

Use the "pulley rein" to regain control of a runaway. Hold one rein tightly, brace on the neck, and pull the other rein straight up and toward you. You should be leaning back, and sitting deep in the saddle.

request to turn. You may have to reach down right to the bit to get a response. The *pulley rein* is useful in this situation. Brace one rein and hand on the neck. Pull up and back on the other rein at the same time (photos 6.1 A & B).

If you're in an indoor arena, you can turn your horse's head toward the wall. This is a bit tricky and should only be used if you're confident and experienced. If you're outside, and you possess a good "feel," you can aim the animal at a fence, but if panicked enough, he may well attempt to jump the fence or run through it. Obviously, these aren't solutions to the problem itself—simply a survival guide.

If you have the skills to force your horse to halt in short order when he bolts, then you have an effec-tive way to manage this problem. These tactics may help you. However, if you can't stop your horse quickly in these circumstances, both of your lives are in danger. If this is a recurring problem, you need to sell the animal, even if a more experienced rider can handle him. The consequences are simply too grave.

Remember that most bad habits develop because of a negative experience or by improper handling. Horses often learn things we don't wish to teach them. Pay attention to the little things about your horse. Don't let him take your space or push you around. Don't encourage his bad habits by letting him have his way when he misbehaves. Don't offer treats or praise to try to calm or bribe him after bad behavior.

Dealing with bad habits often requires confidence and a high degree of skill. You can never make a bad habit disappear, you can only make it fade to the background, and you need to manage the problem so that it *stays* in the background. Failing to remember this will cause the problem to resurface.

Often, when people send their problem horse away for a professional to "fix," the problem comes back a short time later. It's not that the professional didn't do his job. He found a way to make the problem subside, but the owner undid the work. Try to take honest stock of yourself. You need to use common sense, and make sure your ego doesn't overpower your brain. If you use an assistant, make sure he's competent enough to be of help (but try to avoid the "know it all," who may well confuse the issue more).

I have often used, and helped others use, the suggestions offered in this chapter very successfully, but *nothing* works one hundred percent of the time. No quick fixes or magic bullets exist. You need skill and strategy, combined with consistent work.

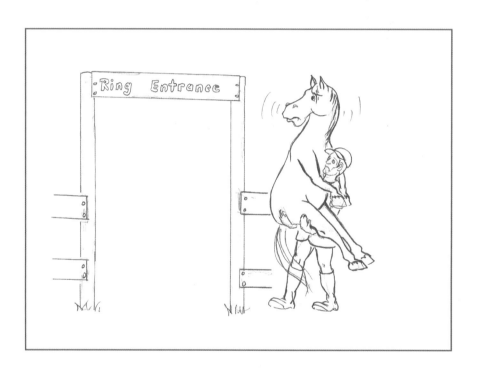

CHAPTER 7

Bombproofing Day

Although bombproofing is an ongoing process that is largely accomplished through daily training with real life obstacles, I *do* conduct actual "bombproofing sessions" for police horses. I also give clinics for the general public that mimic these sessions. A typical session involves schooling multiple horses and riders over many different obstacles and can be held in an indoor arena, outside, or both.

Riding in one of these sessions can be extremely rewarding. It can serve to habituate your horse to many different obstacles in a short period, and can dramatically increase both your mount's confidence and your own. A session can also be used to accustom your horse to a specific task, such as preparing him to carry a flag in a parade. In this chapter, I'll explain exactly how I arrange my own clinics and police horse training, so you can use it as a guideline for a session with a group of friends or on your own with a helper or two.

PLANNING AND PREPARATION

Step 1

Organize some friends. Find several friends with horses they'd like to train who'll join you for the day. You also need to find several other helpers who'll stay on the ground to assist as needed. The ground workers will set up the obstacles (or change them), and aid the riders with their horses. Spouses and children work well for this purpose.

Step 2

Decide what obstacles or situations you would like to use to train. An obstacle can be simple but scary, like a piece of plastic, or as elaborate as a smoke machine. When considering obstacles, your imagination is your only limit (well, maybe your wallet, too). Of course, you should make the obstacles safe. You want to be sure a horse or rider isn't injured if a horse's hoof knocks, steps on, or bumps into one. This will obviously take some planning and preparation.

Most of the obstacles I typically use in my clinics aren't obstacles a horse will have to deal with in his everyday life. I can hardly imagine a situation where *any* horse would be required to traipse over a mattress. However, schooling your horse over mattresses is nonetheless extremely beneficial. When your mount learns to cross a mattress, he learns many lessons. He may remember that you asked him to perform a task that initially frightened him, but that in the end, he had to confront his fear and go where you asked. He may remember that what you asked didn't hurt him. He may also remember that he had at least one experience where he tread on a squishy, soft thing without being harmed. This memory may give him the confidence to obey you when you ask him to tread through mucky, deep footing, or march past a funny looking object.

The same thing is true of schooling your horse to the sound of gunfire (blanks, of course). Maybe you never would consider shooting a gun, either aboard a horse, or on the ground. Perhaps as far as you're concerned, a gun is an object that has no place in your life or that of your equine. But that's not the point. The point is that gunfire is loud and sudden. If you can teach your horse to tolerate *it*, it will increase his tolerance for all sudden, dramatic noises—backfires from cars, for example. This, in turn, will make him more confident. A confident horse that does his job without fear is always more pleasant and safer to ride.

Much of what your horse learns in one lesson will transfer to another. That's why we subject him to fans blowing streamers, smoke bombs, and plastic tarps. If he learns to tackle these problems with aplomb, he will probably tackle almost any problem you want him to. Even if he's not perfect, these exercises will certainly improve him.

So, choose whichever obstacles sound fun.

Step 3

What to do if you can't find friends to school with, or if you just want to train with one obstacle instead of many. You may decide to keep your bombproofing session simple and work on only one obstacle— like accustoming your mount to bicycles if he dislikes them—and that's certainly okay. The format I'm outlining is easy to adjust to your specific situation, and if you do decide to do a session at home, be sure you have at least one person on the ground to help you. However, I'm going to go over how to work on multiple obstacles in a group situation, because this is what I generally do in my clinics.

THE GENERAL SCHOOLING PLAN

The general plan is this: When you and the other riders are comfortable in the new surroundings, you'll begin to school the obstacles. The obstacles will be minimized at first, so even the worst horse in the group can experience success. You repeat schooling over obstacles in their easiest form until both horse and rider are confident. At that point, the obstacles can be made more difficult. Finally, you can move on to other obstacles.

Step 1

Have the ground people set up an obstacle. The ground persons will start by setting up only one obstacle, even if you've chosen five for the training session. They should know exactly how you want it arranged, so you don't have to dismount and change anything once the schooling has begun.

Step 2

Warm up your horse before beginning the schooling session. You and the other riders begin with a little warm-up in the ring to accustom your mounts to the surroundings. When the horses have settled, you can begin schooling the obstacles.

Step 3

School the obstacles:

Minimize the Intensity of Each Obstacle

Since your goal is to find ways to use progressive training for each situation, you'll need to figure out how to minimize the intensity of each obstacle and *set it up at the lowest level.* Later in this chapter, I'll list the ways I do this with the obstacles I typically use. You'll want to read through this section to help you plan which obstacles to choose. If you decide to use an obstacle I haven't included, *you'll* have to figure out how to minimize it.

This is the golden rule: You need to make the obstacles easy enough in the beginning so that *all* the horses are assured of success. Group training should always be started in relation to the worst horse. The horse that trembles when asked to hop over a pole on the ground needs to become confident traversing it before he is asked to try a bigger log. The rider clinging to her horse's neck needs to start simply, within her *comfort zone,* if she hopes to survive an encounter with a smoke bomb. Even if *your* horse acts totally bored with the narrow tarp (and you know you could have started with it all the way open), have patience. You'll eventually get to the highest intensity.

One way to minimize the intensity of an obstacle is to manipulate it. I'll use the tarp as an example (photos 7.1 A to D). Let's say your tarp is ten by twenty feet. If you laid it out to its full size, many of the horses (and riders) might find it difficult to

garner the courage to scramble over it. To minimize its difficulty, you can simply fold it so it's scaled down to about *two* by twenty feet.

When the tarp is this narrow, the horses can easily step over it. They aren't forced to put even one hoof on it. Nevertheless, every time they cross it, they build confidence and courage. When the horses seem comfortable navigating the tarp at its narrowest—whether it takes one repetition or twenty—it can be opened progressively, until it's at its maximum width.

Many times minimizing an obstacle's intensity simply means altering your approach. An example of this would be circling around a frightening thing, so your mount has a chance to adjust to it over the course of a few minutes, instead of forcing him to march straight up to it. Various ways to change your angle of approach are covered extensively in Chapter Four, *Bombproofing Strategies.*

Increasing the distance between your horse and the obstacle can also be an effective way to lessen its difficulty. I'll use a smoke bomb as an example. If you ask your horse to walk between it and the wall of the arena, the task will certainly be easier if you leave thirty feet, instead of merely three. As always, the difficulty can be increased as each horse and rider team is successful. After all of them gain confidence, the distance can be lessened. The horses may well end the session readily treading inches from the smoke bomb.

Find Your Horse's Comfort Zone and Breach It

Find your horse's *comfort zone,* and then don't be afraid to breach it. Obviously, the *way* you push your horse past a level where he's comfortable will differ using different obstacles. If you are asking your mount to trek past a fan blowing streamers, you might ask him to step closer to it than he would

7.1 A—D
The Tarp

A. *To begin training with the tarp, start with it folded into a narrow strip. You can keep it in place when the horse walks on it and when it's windy with traffic cones.*

B. *After the horse is comfortably working over the narrow strip, widen the tarp gradually.*

C. *Repeat the exercise, first working in the horse's comfort zone, then breaching it by opening the tarp up to make it wider and more difficult.*

D. *Now this horse, Baldwin, is walking over the fully opened tarp. Be careful when using large, lightweight tarps as they might get caught on the horse's shoes and be dragged.*

like. If you are trying to get him used to plastic, this might mean pushing him to step over a folded piece. Remember, every horse's fear level and *comfort zone* is unique. What is challenging for one horse might not be for another.

Even with the obstacles minimized, you are likely to find a point past which your horse is uncomfortable proceeding. But he needs to learn to cope. Say, for example, the plastic is only six inches wide and your horse still wants nothing to do with it. This is normal and a part of the learning process. You'll probably need to push to get him through the barriers of his fear.

Most horses—even normally well-behaved ones—will display some type of reaction to stressful situations. Remember my experience with Hollywood? Even a horse that could qualify for sainthood may try to dump you and take off when he's confronted with a fan blowing streamers toward his face.

Try to relax. Here are some hints to help you cope with your horse's undesirable reactions:

He Just Won't Go

General balking or refusing to go forward is a common reaction. If your mount wants to stop and assess a question, let him. Often, if you just keep your aids on your horse, this will be enough to convince him to continue after a moment. You can always push him forward on a circle if he refuses to do so toward an obstacle. Keeping him moving, or even trotting, will help give him the confidence to negotiate the obstacle.

He's Trying to Kill You!

Chapter Six, *Dealing With Bad Habits & Nasty Tricks*, covers most of the techniques you'll need to help you thwart the naughty evasions your horse may use to try and avoid the aforementioned fans.

He's Just Making You Nervous

Let your horse react—it's part of the learning process. He'll settle down once he sees that you're not upset and that he has remained unharmed. Try to give your horse confidence by being confident yourself.

He Tests the Surface

When asked to cross a "walk-over" obstacle, many horses want to test the surface first. Usually, they accomplish this by pawing, sniffing, or looking. This measured assessment is a good thing, as long as it doesn't progress to running the other way. Try to keep your horse facing the obstacle.

He Jumps the Obstacle

When your horse gathers his courage up enough to try to traverse this type of obstacle, you should expect him to jump it. It's certainly not a normal equine reaction for a horse to quietly shuffle over something spooky, so keep your heels down and your eyes focused where you want to go. Remember to stay determined and act like the "leader of the herd," sure of where you want to go and what you want to do.

Leaping the obstacle the first time is a particularly common reaction for a naturally "forward" horse. Your horse may startle when he initially touches the obstacle and *then* jump. In any case, your horse's movements can be very sudden.

If your horse jumps the obstacle, immediately turn him around and cross it again. Many times, when I ask riders to do this, they feel compelled to make a twenty-meter circle first. This is a mistake. *Immediately* means just that. Don't get too far from the obstacle, or your mount may not want to return. The closer you stay, the easier it will be to cross it again. Each pass should produce less reaction, but you don't want to stop until your horse settles down and stops jumping.

7.2 A—C
Herd Instinct

A. *After the smoke bomb is lit, it hisses, and thick smoke starts to rise. This caused some of the horses on the left to shy all together.*

He Bolts Forward When Midway Across the Obstacle
When crossing a walk-over obstacle, your horse may well decide that midway across the obstacle he has reached the point of no return. Typically, at that point, the animal will rush through suddenly. Try to anticipate this reaction so that your bottom is still in the saddle when you reach the other side.

Other techniques you can use to get the horse over—or close to—the obstacles:

Use the "Herd Instinct"
As the group navigates the obstacles, it will quickly become obvious which animals are the bravest. Use them to negotiate the problems first. Their courage will help reassure the skittish horses. Herd instinct is a powerful training tool.

Photos 7.2 A to C show the *herd instinct* at work. In the first photograph, you can see how all the horses on the left were shying away from the terrifying object—in this case, a smoke bomb. However, as they begin to work, they all gain confidence from each other and work through the problem.

Sometimes people in my clinics are concerned that instead of the brave horses influencing the chickens, the chickens will unnerve the rest of the group. Although an overwrought animal never lends confidence to the group—and anytime one truly "blows a gasket" the others are sure to notice—in my experience, the majority of time, the braver ones dominate the situation. If one horse does manage to scare the others, it is often short-lived, particularly when the riders maintain their composure. *Your* calm attitude can go a long way in restoring your mount's composure.

There are subtle techniques to using the brave horse as a leader successfully. Though having

B. Moving the horses in a circle around the smoke bomb helps them keep their attention on their riders' aids. Also, the braver horses help comfort the more nervous ones—a positive use of the herd instinct in training.

C. Here, the horses calmly go through the smoke bomb, one at a time.

When working with almost any obstacle, a brave horse can be used to help train a nervous horse. In this photo, the rider on the braver horse holds the cheek piece of the nervous horse and leads him over the tarp. After some successful passes like this, have the nervous horse follow the braver one, then ask him to cross the tarp on his own.

one horse follow another to gain confidence is a reasonably simple undertaking, I can give you some simple hints to make it as easy as possible.

First, the distance between the leading horse and the skittish one needs to be narrow. Head to tail is best, as close as possible. The rider on the lead horse must pace himself, so that the one following isn't left behind. The lead rider needs to often turn around to check where the skittish one is. To keep the distance closed, he may have to slow to almost a crawl at times, or even halt. Communication between the riders is paramount in this situation. The rider of the skittish horse has to warn the other rider when she's being left and tell the lead rider what she needs. The lead rider won't be able have his head turned the *whole* time.

Sometimes, when following, the timid horse will suddenly respond to the urging of his rider and lurch forward. Going forward—even if it's *lurching*

forward—is a good thing. It means the rider is riding her horse through his reaction. The lead rider needs to be alert enough to get out of the way.

The same rules apply if you are riding side-by-side. Stay next to one another. The rider on the braver horse shouldn't ride away from the other. Let the braver horse take the inside path (closest to the monster). Your horse will feel safer and more secure on the outside because his instincts tell him the monster will eat the other horse before *him*. Remember to change directions, so you train each side of your horse.

Pony the Reluctant Animal

Sometimes the lead rider can *pony* the reluctant animal (photo 7.3). To pony a horse simply means to lead him from the back of another—a common practice at the racetrack. If you are going to do this, you need to ride with one hand, and use the other to lead. I prefer to hold the cheek piece, so the rider can keep her reins. Though this is ideal, sometimes you may have to hold her reins, instead. If you do grasp the reins, be prepared to let go.

Work from the Ground

Working your horse from the ground is another useful way to introduce your horse to some obstacles. This is particularly true of walk-over obstacles, or where a rider is afraid of riding through her mount's initial reaction. There's nothing wrong with making it easy. How to do this is covered in detail in Chapter Five.

Repeat the Obstacle

That you convinced your horse to attempt the obstacle is wonderful. But you're not ready to make the obstacle tougher, or move onto the next one, until he no longer seems challenged by the lowest level.

Some horses need more repetition and training sessions than others, and some even act as if a situation is brand new to them, even if you've previously trained in a similar situation. Take a deep breath. You're the rider; the one that has to have patience. It may take your horse twenty-seven tries over the tarp before he relaxes. You don't want to give up at number twenty-five or twenty-six. Maybe he *does* only have a hamster-sized brain. He's still learning. You have to be more persistent than your horse.

Increase the Intensity

The idea is to gradually increase the intensity of each obstacle. Your mount's *comfort zone* will gradually increase also, through positive reinforcement (patting and praise for his courage and obedience), as well as the repetitions.

Once everyone in your group has successfully worked on an obstacle, you can ask your ground helpers to set up the next one, but leave the first intact.

This way you can go back to it and reinforce your training. Follow the same procedure for the rest of the obstacles. Make sure you leave enough space between them so you can work on each independently.

THE OBSTACLES

Safety Comes First

Besides listing the obstacles I commonly use in my clinics, I'll explain how to *minimize* each of them. Before I start, though, let me remind you that you need to ensure that *whatever* obstacles you decide to use are safe. Try to imagine how a horse or rider could get into trouble. Are there sharp edges to run into? If it breaks, what might happen? If one of the horses punches through one (say a poorly made teeter-totter), there's the danger of a hoof getting stuck or cut. You don't want something heavy or sharp collapsing onto either your friends or their horses. It's a sure way to get taken off a Christmas card list!

When setting up obstacles, remember to use the side of the arena or the wall to your advantage. Many horses want to evade an obstacle by going off to one side. You can eliminate at least one escape route by putting it against the wall.

Occupied Cars, Large Trucks, and Motorcycles

Because they are common everyday sights, most horses are used to vehicles in general. Even high-strung racehorses are usually conditioned to cars because they're exposed to them at the racetrack. However, certain things about them can cause headaches for you. A car driving past your horse may not be a problem, but just try to get him to saunter up to an occupied vehicle to speak to the occupants—that's another situation altogether.

Motorcycles can be intimidating because they're loud. Standing next to one being started can be particularly frightening. Large trucks present problems, because they are visually intimidating and their mechanical functions are noisy as well (air brakes, roll-up doors, huge diesel engines). Mounted police horses have to approach occupied vehicles and walk past trucks everyday, so their being habituated to them is of paramount importance.

How to Set Up and School

To get your horse to approach an occupied vehicle, start with it turned off. Have the driver calmly speak to your horse. It also helps to arm the driver with a treat to give to your horse once he approaches the door. As your horse becomes more poised, you can make this exercise more challenging by turning on the radio and starting the motor. The driver can create distractions by acting animated, too.

If your mount is apprehensive, stroll back and forth, getting closer as you go. Or, as your horse assesses the situation, walk in a circle around the vehicle, gradually spiraling closer. Use the *head away* position to help you. Eventually, you can approach on the driver's door, from either the rear or front of the car.

To accustom your horse to a motorcycle being started next to him, have a helper repeatedly start and rev the motor. Begin this exercise with your horse a good distance away from the motorcycle—in his *comfort zone*—and decrease it as his composure grows.

Bicycles

For some reason, a lot of people's horses seem to have a problem with bicycles. However, in my experience, although many horses that I've worked with have had mild reactions to them, I've never seen what I would consider an extreme reaction.

How to Set Up and School

To get your horse used to bicycles you'll need a helper to jump on a bike and ride around him. If he's really apprehensive, dismount and stand with him. Have your helper circle around him on the bike, gradually getting closer. As usual, how gradual the procedure is, and how close the cyclist comes, is dependent on your horse's reaction.

If you've dismounted, as your horse becomes more confident you'll want to climb into the saddle again and repeat the exercise. Walk your horse in a large circle (like around the perimeter of your riding school) while the bicyclist rides in both directions. Have him approach your mount from the front and behind, too. Obviously, you and the bicyclist need to coordinate the distance that is appropriate for your horse's response (if your mount bolts and screams around the arena ten times, the cyclist has *probably* ridden too close).

The photos 7.4 A to F were taken on a road. When you first introduce the bicycle, you need to be sure the horse has somewhere safe to "escape"—the grassy area at the edge of the road, in this instance.

A

B

C

D

E

F

7.4 A—F
Bicycles

A. *Diane, riding Curly, meets Anne riding her bicycle. They start this training with plenty of distance between Curly and the bicycle, and leave Curly plenty of room to "escape" onto grass before reaching a narrow bridge. Since he shows no negative reaction, they all continue and cross the bridge.*

B. *After getting safely over the bridge, Diane lets Curly investigate and sniff Anne's bicycle. Diane gives his shoulder a pat as a reward.*

C. *Now, the distance is decreased between the horse and bicycle. Curly looks closely, but shows no adverse reaction to the bicycle getting closer. Diane and Anne communicate so Curly can hear something behind him.*

D. *Repeat this exercise going back and forth over the bridge. As you do when training with other obstacles, always work from both directions.*

E. *Curly does a good job, so once again he is brought up close to the bicycle where he receives a reward.*

F. *Curly now allows the bicycle to come right up beside him while he stands on the grass.*

Road Flares
Where to Get Them

Auto supply stores are a reliable source for these. They make an interesting obstacle because of the visual stimulus they provide—they're scary to look at. They also produce a little smoke and smell, so they're scary to sniff. Finally, they hiss, so they sound scary, too. Since they could have well been designed to offend most of your horse's senses, they make a particularly useful obstacle to school.

How to Set Up and School

A flare should be set at a forty-five degree angle, always pointed away from the track. This is because you don't want the flame to spit at the horse that gets close to it, thus punishing him for obeying. If your horse scorches his fetlocks when he finds enough courage to finally step close, the training will be counterproductive, to say the least.

During a clinic, I usually set the flares up on the edge of the ring, around its perimeter, as in Photos 7.5 A & B. You can *minimize the intensity* of this obstacle with distance. Some horses may be comfortable moving only five feet away. Others may need twenty feet or more. You'll find *your* horse's *comfort zone* by gauging his reaction. If your horse is shying and facing the flare, and you can't push him past it, his reaction *should* tell you you've come too close. Although you may need to

7.5 A—B

Road Flares

A. *These riders and horses establish their own individual comfort zone from the road flares.*

B. *A successful pass—quite close to the flares.*

start more conservatively, using the *head away* can help convince your horse to saunter by without the antics.

Gradually, as he gains confidence, get your horse closer. Remember to work both directions. The next step is to set the flares up so that you have to walk *between* them. Twenty feet apart is a good distance to begin with, but as usual, the horses themselves will dictate the distance necessary. Then have your ground helpers gradually put them closer together as you train.

Cage Balls
Where to Get Them

Cage balls are large, inflatable balls that measure five to six feet in diameter (see *Appendix*). Caution: Do not leave them unattended in hot weather as they are sensitive to temperature and can possibly burst. In Chapter Four, page 70, I outlined how to do a spiraling exercise to get your horse close to the cage ball. Now we'll go a step further and do some work (as well as play) with it.

How to Set Up and School

The objective is to get your horse to become comfortable pushing the ball, and eventually, tolerate it coming toward him. You need at least one helper on the ground to control the ball.

To start, have your ground person move the ball away from your mount while he approaches it (photos 7.6 A & B). The key is to approach it at a slightly faster rate than it moves away. Since the ball is moving away from your horse, he isn't as likely to see it as a threat.

If the ball is moving *toward* your horse, he'll probably attempt to escape from it. Not only is it weird looking, it's *chasing* him, too. Many horses refuse to get close enough to touch or smell a ball

that stubbornly holds its ground, either. A stationary ball is more intimidating than one that flees.

However, the ball running *from* your horse will build his courage. Eventually, he'll close the distance, and next, he'll begin to brush it with his nose. Since, of course, every mount is different, some will touch the ball sooner than others. You may have to work with yours for a while to get him to this first stage. Remember to use the *herd instinct* to help you. Utilizing a braver horse that's comfortable touching the ball helps lend the apprehensive one confidence.

Some animals push the ball with their heads, chest or shoulders (photo 7.6 C). Some try biting it. It's fun when several horses get involved in an equine "soccer" game (photo 7.6 D).

Once your horse is pushing the ball, you should develop his ability to stand while the ball is pushed *at* him—the most challenging scenario. Start by pulling it away (about six inches) while he's touching it, and then roll it back to him. As long as he is accepting, begin increasing the distance until you can do it from several feet away. Lastly, you should make sure he accepts being touched by the ball all over his body, from head to tail.

Trash Pile: Plastic Bottles, Aluminum Cans, Plastic Cups and Plates, and More
Where to Get Them

The answer is, of course, *anyplace*. If you're looking for cheap, easy, and effective obstacles, plastic bottles, aluminum cans, plastic cups, plates, and "nerf" or foam balls can all be used. When your horse steps over and through them, they make noise. They're perfectly safe, too. I usually place something around the bottles and cans to keep them somewhat contained. Tires work well.

7.6 A—D
The Cage Ball

A. *After spiraling in, the cage ball training begins with the ground person pulling the ball away as Curly and Baldwin approach it.*

B. *When the horses realize the ball isn't going to chase them, they can be encouraged to touch it with their noses or chests. The goal is for the horses to push or move the ball on their own. This becomes a game for the riders as well.*

C. *Curly and Baldwin get into the spirit of the game. They both eagerly work with the ball, and even begin to compete for it.*

D. *Riders participate in a "soccer" game at the end of a training clinic.*

7.7 A—D
The Trash Pile

A. *Start the trash-pile obstacle with a wide, open path for the horse to walk through. This gives him a chance to see what's near him, but does not force him to step on anything.*

B. *Some trash has been added to the path for Jasper to negotiate through. He'll work at this level until he is comfortable.*

C. *More rubbish has been added and the space in the middle made smaller by moving the tires closer, as well. Jasper is negotiating the trash and actually has to step on some of it.*

D. *Always work from both directions, as Jasper does, here. A horse may be confused coming from one direction, but not the other.*

How to Set Up and School
When your ground helper sets up the obstacle, instruct him to leave a path through the objects. It should be wide enough that your horse can easily negotiate it *without* being asked to step on anything strange. Gradually, put some of the objects in the path, so that your horse begins stepping on or over them.

Once your horse shuffles through them without reaction, continue to put more in his path. Soon, he'll be stepping confidently through piles of balls and bottles. Always remember to work in both directions (photos 7.7 A to D).

Plastic Tarps or Rolls of Plastic
Where to Get Them
Your local home improvement center should carry different sizes and varieties of plastic tarps. These, and rolls of black plastic, both have shiny surfaces that can look frightening, and further, make a scary, crinkling noise. Your horse can drag the tarp backward toward himself if he paws it, so prepare to sit tight.

How to Set Up and School
Folding to a smaller size easily minimizes both tarps and rolls of plastic. Schooling over the tarp is used as an example earlier in this chapter (see page 106 and photos 7.1 A to D.)

Nerf Balls
Where to Get Them
Nerf balls are foam, spongy, colorful balls, which can be used to get your horse used to objects coming at him, or even *thrown* at him. They're easily acquired at toy stores or chain discount stores.

How to Set Up and School
To begin, have a helper stroke your horse's neck with the nerf ball. When he accepts this without fuss, your helper can begin to bounce the ball off his neck. Initially, this should be done from a very close distance (six inches or so). Don't forget to have your helper work on both sides. As your horse begins to understand that he's not being hurt, your helper can progress to his front end. Initially, he'll throw the balls gently and low, toward your horse's feet. Gradually, he can throw the balls higher and harder. He'll continue until your mount will tolerate the balls thrown straight toward his face, and also from further away.

To increase your horse's confidence even more, you can ride him forward while your helper walks backward and tosses balls at you. Whenever something flees from your horse, he'll find it less threatening. After all, if it's scared of him, that's more reassuring than if it holds its ground, or worse yet, tries to chase *him* (photos 7.8 A to D).

Fans with Streamers
Where to Get Them
You will need to have an accessible electrical outlet if you decide to use a fan with streamers. Obviously, you should keep the cord out of the picture. You can choose any kind of streamer, ribbon, or other object light enough for the fan to blow.

How to Set Up and School
The objective is to be able to ride your horse past the distraction. You can use the same procedure that you did with the flares, first minimizing its frightening effect by establishing distance between it and your horse. Because you'll probably only have one fan, you'll have to walk by it, and then turn around. Therefore, you alternate between riding by with the fan on one side, then the other. With a "walk-by" obstacle, the most popular evasions used by equines are shying and wheeling.

7.8 A—D Nerf Balls

A. *Start nerf-ball training by aiming low and tossing them one at a time toward the horse's feet.*

B. *The nerf balls are now tossed higher, two at a time, aiming for Curly's chest.*

C. *Throw as many nerf balls as can be held at once—aiming for the chest. If the horse backs away, bring him back into place and keep at it.*

D. *Here, Curly is having trouble with so many nerf balls landing on and near him. However, Diane is able to keep him from moving away. Lots of praise and pats are given for Curly's good job.*

7.9 A—E
Balloons

A. To start, the balloons are set far apart so the horse has a clear path between them.

B. The path between the balloons is narrowed, and Curly is worked in both directions until he is comfortable.

Balloons
Where to Get Them

You can get helium-inflated balloons from many grocery stores or specialty "party" stores. "Mylar" balloons are less likely to pop; latex balloons will pop if it's windy and when they touch blades of grass. In the accompanying photographs, two ground people are holding latex balloons, and mylar ones are close to the ground.

How to Set Up and School

Keep in mind that wind will be a factor in determining how difficult an obstacle is on any given day because balloons bumping into each other and jumping in the breeze are certainly more visually and auditorily threatening to the horse. Tie the balloons onto any kind of stable object—PVC pipe, drainage pipes (as in the photograph), jump standards, boards, and so forth.

Photos 7.9 A to E show how to work through this obstacle. In the beginning, set up balloons on parallel lines fairly wide apart—wide enough so that the your horse will negotiate the obstacle willingly, within his *comfort zone*. We started out about twenty feet wide. As horse and rider progressed, it became more challenging as the distance between the lines of balloons closed and the horse had to negotiate a narrow passage.

C. The balloons are getting closer, but Curly remains calm as he negotiates the pathway.

D. The balloons are so close that Curly is intimidated. Diane lets him look and investigate before asking him to move forward.

E. With the balloon obstacle at its most difficult, Curly now easily negotiates his way through.

Wooden Bridges or Teeter-Totters
Where to Get Them

I've always made this obstacle, which can be fun, and not too difficult. To construct a bridge, use four-by-fours, or six-by-sixes, depending on the height you want. Make sure there is center support for your bridge so you don't end up training your mount to stay off such a dangerous surface, instead of on it. Cover it with thick plywood or pressure-treated boards.

To make it a teeter-totter, place a pole or four-by-four underneath your bridge. When your horse walks forward, the bridge will tip to the front.

How to Set Up and School

Schooling this obstacle is similar to schooling the tarp, so look for similar evasions and reactions. The difference is you can't manipulate the size of the bridge, and it's elevated. Therefore, you have to initially make the training easier by varying your approach. You can begin by having your horse cross its width. If the bridge is two- or even three-by-six-feet wide, he can easily jump it. Once he's comfortable with crossing its width, he can begin crossing its length.

Another way to accustom your horse to the situation is simply to start by riding him over a sheet of plywood, before introducing him to the bridge. *After your horse has gained confidence over this "static bridge," you can introduce the teeter-totter aspect.*

7.10
Mattresses

Curly is asked to walk the shortest distance across the mattress. He is allowed to examine it.

Mattresses

Where to Get Them

Mattresses are challenging walk-over obstacles, because they *give* when stepped on. Your horse will require lots of confidence not only in himself, but also in *you*, to successfully tackle this test. If you don't have an old mattress you can recycle, check the classifieds. People often give them away.

How to Set Up and School

Place the mattress so the horse will negotiate the narrowest, easiest way first (photo 7.10). In the beginning, if the horse refuses to get close enough to touch or sniff the mattress, you should simply make repeated passes near it until you can get him close enough to sniff it or touch it with a foot. If the horse attempts to walk around and not over it, you will need to place one side of the mattress next to a wall or fence. Keep the horse focused on the mattress—sometimes ground poles or traffic cones will help to keep his attention. Please refer to Chapter Three, page 51, where I showed you how I introduced a horse to the mattress obstacle, first in hand, and then mounted.

Two mattresses also work well. Place them next to each other, with the long sides parallel, and leave a three-foot space in between. If your mount objects to treading on the mattresses, you can ride between them. As you continue, attempt to get him to brush against the mattresses as you move between them.

Your goals for schooling this obstacle should be consistent with those you have for the other walk-over obstacles. You have been productive if your horse will touch the mattress, step on, sniff, and assess it. Then, he should be asked to cross its width—the shortest distance across. Remember, you can always start in hand, and then mount up. Be prepared for the horse to jump the obstacle the first few times—this is a fine way to start, because at least he crossed it.

As your horse gains in confidence, you can continue to make this obstacle more and more challenging. You can ask your horse to cross lengthwise and lay a mat on top (photos 7.11 A & B). Continue to add new elements, like balloons, to increase its difficulty (photos 7.11 C to E).

7.11 A—E

Increase the Difficulty of the Mattress Obstacle

A & B. This horse is carefully crossing the mattress lengthwise. The obstacle is made more difficult with the addition of a mat on top.

7.11 A—E cont.

Increase the Difficulty of the Mattress Obstacle

C. To increase the difficulty even further, you can add balloons beside the mattress.

D & E. The balloons have been moved closer to the mattress, and the horse is taking it all in stride.

7.12 A & B

The Smoke Bomb

A. *Light the smoke bomb after everyone is walking calmly in a large circle. When the smoke bomb is lit, it will hiss, produce thick smoke, and smell. Try to keep walking, and begin to spiral in toward the center. The object is to have your horse walk through the thick haze.*

Smoke and Smoke Machines

Although smoke is used to train police horses for the specific purpose of acclimating them to things used in crowd control, general training benefits exist, as well. From this type of work, your horse learns that he can walk *through* smoke—something that he views as a solid wall. Most smoke grenades also make a hissing noise, and of course, they smell.

Where to Get Them

Most music stores sell smoke machines—disc jockeys and bands often use them. Keep in mind that the "smoke" from smoke machines is a lot more like steam: it has a pleasant smell and can certainly be used indoors. On the downside, the ones that you buy from music stores will have an electric cord, so they can't be circled safely, and because the smoke is intermittent, you won't have absolute control over the discharge.

Another option is a smoke grenade with a fuse, typically used to find leaks in pipes (see *Appendix*, p. 175).

Finally, the cheapest and most easily available option is to make a pile of hay or straw and light it. Obviously, be sure you're doing so on an approved burn day and in a safe area; and of course, be very careful in such situations.

How to Set Up and School

It's hard to control smoke. The weather and wind will largely decide how your obstacle will appear. On a windy day, the smoke will generally disperse quickly and will stay low to the ground as it blows. Often, when it floats close to the ground, your horse will try to jump it. On less windy days, smoke will look like a wall that your horse believes he can't penetrate. Minimize the intensity of this obstacle by circling the source of the smoke at a comfortable distance. As you circle, you can progressively get nearer (photos 7.12 A & B).

7.12 A & B cont.
The Smoke Bomb

B. Don't force your horse to get close to the center of the circle too quickly. If your horse startles, ease off by putting him back in his comfort zone, and keep moving. Once he has settled, start the spiral-in again. Ultimately, try to get your horse to walk through the smoke.

Carrying Flags

Carrying flags on horseback looks impressive. However, if your mount bolts from the parade and gallops off in the other direction when you pick one up, the effect is certainly somewhat lessened. Getting your horse used to this task can sometimes be a challenge. On a windy day, flags blow around, making all kinds of noise, and sometimes even covering your horse's head.

Where to Get Them

Flags can be purchased from chain discount stores or at Flags Unlimited Inc. at www.usflags.com. For those with even basic sewing skills, practice flags can be homemade. They are much cheaper than purchased parade flags, and you don't need to worry about dropping them on the ground. My flags are made from nylon material and measure 4½ by 3 feet. Here are the steps for assembly:

1 Fold and sew all the edges of the material so it doesn't fray.

2 Fold and sew one of the short ends to accommodate a one-inch-diameter pole. Don't make it too tight because the flag needs to slide easily through.

3 Next, create another strip of fabric about 1 by 2 inches in size and attach it to two sides of the opening where the pole will go (photo 7.13).

4 Slide a metal key ring onto the fabric loop you have just made.

5 Cut a piece of PVC pipe (plastic plumber's pipe) 1 inch in diameter and about 8½ feet long. This is your flagpole. Slide your flag onto the pole.

7.13
A Homemade Flag
Instructions for assembly are on this page.

About 1½ inches from the end of the pipe, drill a guide hole that is slightly smaller than the screw end of a common screw eye, then insert a screw eye into the pipe.

6 Lastly, attach the key ring to the screw eye to secure the flag on the pole.

How to Set Up and School

In the worst-case scenario, your horse may be nervous just getting near the flag. If this is the situation, start by standing to the near side of him. Hold the cheek piece of his bridle (or the side of his halter) with your left hand. Taking the flag in your right hand, begin touching your horse on the neck with it. If he tries to run away, just turn him in a circle. Allow your horse to pace around you as you continue rubbing.

After a while (maybe twenty-five or thirty touches), your horse will settle down. You'll know he's starting to relax when you see him look away.

Continue until he stands quietly, tolerating the flag with confidence. Continue down and around his entire near side, then change sides, and repeat.

To get your horse accustomed to the flag while it's *attached* to the pole, you'll need assistance. Duplicate the procedure previously described, but as you touch your horse with the flag, have a ground helper stand behind you and hold the pole. Many times, horses are more concerned about the pole than the flag, so make sure your helper keeps the pole as low and as far away as possible. Your helper will have to stay close to you, and move with you if you circle (photos 7.14 A to C).

Once your mount accepts the flag, you'll need to repeat the exercise with the pole itself. Touch and stroke your horse with the flag-wrapped pole in one hand. Your other hand will control your horse's head, just as it did when you accustomed him to the flag.

The next step is to *carry* the flag. Traditionally, the flag is carried in your right hand, but you should get your horse used to it on both sides. I use several methods to train horses to do this. However, before you begin to experiment with any of them, tie your reins in a knot, so you're not juggling extra rein material (see p. 169).

One of the methods you can begin with is to ride your horse with a helper walking next to you with the flag. This is useful because it simulates the rider (you) carrying the flag without you having to actually hold it. Your horse is conditioned to the flag, but in the meantime, *you* have control of him.

At first, your helper should hold the flag so it's *not* flying freely. Let your horse get used to this. Your assistant can let it loose in small increments. Use

distance to *minimize the threat*. As your horse's *comfort zone* increases, close the distance.

Once the horse is used to the flag, have the ground person hand it up to you. Have your helper continue walking next to your horse until you're sure he's relaxed. As you gain confidence, begin to let the flag fly on its own. If you get into trouble, simply hand it back to your helper. When both you and your mount are breathing normally, you can step away on your own (photos 7.15 A to F).

You can also use a horse-and-rider team that is already able to carry a flag to train your animal. To start, ride next to the experienced team while they carry a flag. Again, at first the flag should be held close to the staff to prevent it from blowing. It can be released in increments as your horse relaxes, and the distance you've established can be closed up (photos 7.16 A to C).

After your horse is settled, you can have the rider on the experienced horse hand the flag to you. When this is accomplished successfully, you can let the flag fly (photos 7.16 D & E). If your horse goes ballistic, simply drop the flag on the ground. Expect him to lurch away from it as you drop it. If you try to grab the reins and hold onto the flag, you may hit the horse with the flagpole. I *have* seen it happen. This is where riding with one hand is absolutely necessary. Eventually, both of you will be able to ride side-by-side, each carrying a flag, and eventually join other horses that have been trained to carry flags in formation (photos 7.16 F to H).

If you plan to work extensively with flags, in preparation for a parade, for example, invest in a flag holder (see *Appendix*, p. 175).

7.14 A—C
Introducing Flags

A. *This horse doesn't want to be close to the flag. He wants to run away but is restricted to running in a circle around me. When he calms down, I shorten the lead line to bring him gradually closer to the flag.*

B. *After the horse is walking calmly around me, an assistant is called in to hold the flagpole. I then actually rub the horse with the flag, as if I were grooming him. This settles the horse down and he becomes more accepting of it.*

C. *Now the horse is very comfortable with the flag— even when it is blowing over, and on, him.*

7.15 A—F
Training with Flags

A. *Flag training is started with a ground person carrying a flag a short distance from the horse's shoulder, just in front of the rider's leg. This allows the horse to get used to the flag being near him. The ground person should not let the flag fly at this time. The horse needs to become accustomed to one thing at a time—first, just a flag, and second, a flapping flag.*

B. *I am walking closer to the horse, still holding the flag so that it doesn't fly.*

C. *While standing, prepare to raise flag so that the rider can pick it up and place it on her boot or in a flag holder.*

D. *I hand the flag to Diane who raises it up high enough to place the pole on top of her boot. If Curly gets excited, Diane will simply let go of the pole, which I'm holding too, and deal with her horse.*

E. *Here, Diane places the flagpole on her toe. Curly is steady, so training continues.*

F. *With the flag flying on this windy day, Diane is pleased that Curly has adapted to it successfully. He can now be used to train another horse.*

7.16 A—H

Adding Flags and Horses

A. *While walking, the new horse is asked to stay close to Curly's shoulder and the flag.*

B. *Once this new horse is comfortable walking next to the flag, the rider prepares to carry it.*

C. *Here, the new horse allows his rider to take the flag and place it on her toe. In fact, the horse probably doesn't realize who is carrying the flag—he just sees it's there and it doesn't bother him.*

D. *The flag is slowly released and allowed to fly. If the horse has a problem, the rider simply drops the flag and deals with her horse. Both riders should keep an eye on the flag at all times.*

E & F. *A successful training session! We now have two horse-and-rider teams with flying flags.*

**7.16 A—H con't.
Adding Flags and
Horses**

*G & H. There are four
trained horse-and-rider
teams with flags. Now,
I'm starting formation
work, where all four
ride with flags in a
straight line. This type
of training is very useful
for parade work.*

Giggle Balls

Giggle balls are battery-operated plastic balls that bounce, tumble, and make a loud giggly noise. They're great to get your horse used to unexpected sound and movement—such as animals leaping out from the underbrush.

Where to Get Them

Giggle balls can be bought at most toy stores and many chain discount stores.

How to Set Up and School

First, you must construct a frame (wooden or otherwise) to prevent the giggle balls from tumbling across the training field and disappearing forever in the woods. As soon as you turn them on, they begin to bounce and tumble; they stop for a moment, giggle, and suddenly start up again. Horses seem to do better in a group for this obstacle, so be sure to use the *herd instinct* to your advantage. Once the first horse will walk close to the giggle balls, the others will follow (photos 7.17 A & B).

7.17 A & B
Giggle Balls

A. *Giggle balls, which bounce, tumble and make loud, "giggling" noises, prove to be quite mysterious to horses. However, riders find them comical, and laughter may calm horses.*

B. *Here, the herd instinct takes over. With a brave horse standing close to the bouncing balls, other horses move in to see what's going on.*

7.18 A—D

The Noodle Wall

A. With a ground person holding the noodles back, this rider is trotting her horse through the noodle wall.

B. After a few passes, this horse goes through on his own.

C. Now, the chestnut horse is led through the noodles.

D. Later, he walks calmly through with his rider on board.

The Noodle Wall

Just like a car going through a carwash, this exercise teaches your horse to go *through* unknown territory, and it makes fighting through heavy brush (if you ever want to take your horse camping, for example) or densely wooded areas, a breeze.

Where to Get Them

For the frame, visit your local hardware store and pick up three sections of straight PVC pipe (two-inch minimum in diameter, with a minimum length of eight feet) and two PVC elbows. You also need two five-gallon buckets, a bag of concrete, and some duct tape. For the "noodles," pick up some fishing line and a variety of toys or small objects to hang off the frame. I often use Styrofoam pool toys, which don't get tangled or blow around.

Set each upright section in the center of a bucket while another person pours in the concrete a little at a time. You can mix it in the bucket as you go if you like, just don't put in too much water. The person holding the upright will need to keep it centered and use a level to make sure it is plumb. Tape the pipes securely with the duct tape; let it set until the concrete is dry. Then lay the pipes on the ground and attach the elbows. Attach the fishing line to the objects/toys, and slide each noodle on the crosspiece.

How to Set Up and School

Begin by pushing half the noodles to each side, leaving a large opening for your horse to pass through easily. Gradually close up the noodles so your horse has to push against them. If you're working several horses simultaneously, it often helps to leave two spaces open—so there's a hard way and an easy way, depending on the horse's level (photos 7.18 A to D).

Firing Blanks

Gunfire is always a difficult issue to confront—for both horses and humans. The explosion is often very loud and very unexpected: it's bad enough when we're prepared for it, but it can be terrifying when we don't know it's coming. For a horse, it can be even more terrifying, especially since many horses have grown up never hearing the sound.

Exposing your horse to gunfire has many great benefits, even if you don't anticipate that your horse will *ever* hear a real gun. Your horse will certainly hear loud, unexpected noises—thunder, a window shattering, a car backfiring, construction noises, and so forth—in his lifetime. Also, knowing and being able to predict your horse's reaction when he's confronted with a loud noise can make you more effective at managing his response.

The great aspect about accustoming a horse to gunfire is that, while training your horse, you are able to manage and control the loud sound. You can choose the time, place, and frequency, so you can really work with, and work through, his reaction.

Where to Get Them

For accustoming a horse to loud noises, use a so-called "starter's pistol," the kind of gun that's used to start races. They can be purchased at a sporting goods store, and there's no chance of getting injured because the barrel is false and can never hold a projectile.

How to Set Up and School

Training for gunfire works better if you acclimate several horses to it at the same time. You and your friends should start by having your horses walk in a circle. Since your horses are already moving forward, their reactions will be more easily controlled. Moving tends to help horses be less anxious than forcing them to stand.

7.19
Gunfire

After the smoke-bomb obstacle, gunfire from a starter's pistol is introduced to the group. If the group can tolerate the sound, the blanks are fired from a closer distance, thereby making this noise obstacle louder.

Creating space between your mount and the gunfire is the way to reduce this problem's intensity. Fifty yards away is a good distance to start with, but you still need to appraise your horse's reactions after the first shot. If you have to go further out, do so. You'll see in photo 7.19 how far away the horses are from the gun when it's first fired. In this photograph, the cloud behind the horses is the remains of a smoke-bomb from a different test, not smoke from the gun.

Gradually, the person firing the gun can get closer—as long as the horses appear to accept it. Typically, the horses will startle initially. Some drop down suddenly, others spin to look at the source of the explosion, and some just scoot away without bothering to take the time to look—they *know* they don't want to be near anything that loud.

Usually, the reactions last only seconds. Since the noise from the gun is very brief, your horse will probably return to strolling along by the time you are centered again in the saddle. As the gun continues to fire, your horse and the others will react less and less, until they remain walking calmly. Some may even be able to stand quietly. Have your ground helper shoot only as close as the worst horse in your clinic can comfortably tolerate. If habituating your horse to gunfire is important to you, you should repeat this procedure regularly. Most horses improve greatly with regular exposure.

Combining Obstacles

Balloons, tires, and traffic cones all make interesting tests. You can also make obstacles more difficult by

7.20
Combining Obstacles

Here, we combine many different obstacles: mattress, mat, balloons, and flags. On top of this, it is a very windy day, which adds yet another difficult element.

combining them. Photo 7.20 shows a combined obstacle. The horse and rider are crossing the mattress lengthwise (the hard way), with a painted mat draped over it, and blowing balloons and flags flanking it. Remember, as long as obstacles are safe, your imagination is the limit.

Other Hints

Habituating a police horse is a bit different than habituating the average horse. That difference is that the police horse, while on patrol, is being exposed to things for six-to-eight-hour periods, day in and out.

Let's say your horse has a problem with bicycles. Maybe you've schooled him three or four times with them, and he still hasn't figured out that they don't intend to eat him. Now, imagine your horse spending an entire day on a bike path—even an entire *week* there. After a couple of days, bicycles would be no problem at all.

If you get frustrated while schooling your horse, this is important to remember. Sometimes, it may take a while for your horse to get over his fear. The average person may be able to steal an hour or two a few days a week to train, so the process will naturally take longer.

Making the Day into a Competition

It can make for a fun situation if you and your friends get together and have a little good-natured contest—a bombproof competition, if you will. To do this, set a series of obstacles up around an enclosed area. Then, one at a time, you can enter the area and try to tackle the course you set.

7.21 A & B
Soccer Game

A. *A treat for horses and riders after a training session is to play "soccer." The ball may simply be pushed around, or goalposts set up and teams picked. Make up your own rules.*

This kind of event can actually help school your animal, and it's important to make sure he'll enter the arena by himself, too. Many times, when your horse resists in this kind of situation, the problem is his *herd instinct, not* the obstacles. He may be happy to face a smoke bomb—*if* you can wrench him away from his buddies.

Establish objectives for each obstacle. For instance, if you have a bridge set up, it's pretty obvious if one of the competitors has been successful in crossing it or not. On the other hand, you need to set a standard boundary distance from an object (think of it as a corridor width) for walking *past* something, such as a fan blowing streamers. The same is true for standing *next* to an obstacle. Use cones, lime, or paint to establish these boundaries, and determine a maximum time frame for each obstacle. Once that time has past, the competitor will be required to move to the next one if she's been unsuccessful negotiating it.

Setting your course up in an open environment can be a interesting challenge, but you'll have to be

B. A good play for goal.

cautious of the loose-horse syndrome. Don't set up near a road or in a place where there could be major problems if a horse gets away. Have responsible ground people to help in case trouble arises.

Another activity that can test your mount is a judged pleasure ride. This sort of competition offers an obstacle course in a trail ride environment— a way to teach your horse and enjoy yourself at the same time.

One of the most entertaining—and rewarding— activities in my clinics is a soccer game with a cage ball—if you have enough horses to divide into two teams. It's a huge amount of fun, and really builds confidence for both the riders and the horses (photos 7.21 A & B). The other really great aspect of a soccer game is that if you leave other obstacles— mattresses, tarps, and so forth—in the arena, the horses and the riders will be so concerned about playing the soccer game, horses that wouldn't get near a mattress will run right over it as they chase the ball.

Robyn

It was my job to teach Robyn, a strapping Thorough-bred gelding with a fuzzy mane and a dressage background, about being a police horse. In one of his early lessons, I set up a variety of objects for him to work over, including a rubber mat that was black with yellow crosswalk stripes. The mat was about ten feet long and maybe thirty inches wide. I thought that it would be a reasonable place to begin our schooling for the day.

When Robyn had warmed up, I rode him toward the mat. To say he didn't want to approach it would be an understatement. First, he planted himself firmly, hooves splayed out in front of him. Next, he snorted and galloped away, ignoring my requests to stop until he felt he had achieved a safe distance.

I considered this a pretty strong reaction, so I dismounted to work him from the ground. Using a restraint over his nose that created pressure when he tried to back away, I gradually encouraged him forward. Finally, he gathered his courage and jumped the mat. After jumping the mat several times, he began to notice that it hadn't actually snapped at his tail on the way over. Bravely, he finally tested it with the tip of a foot.

From there, he progressed quickly. He settled to the point where he could walk, and finally stand, on the mat. Then I mounted Robyn, but he wasn't afraid any more. I had to push him a little, but he managed to duplicate his groundwork while under tack. I felt that it had been a constructive training session that had progressed fairly typically. All was well.

The next day, after we'd warmed up, I again aimed Robyn at the mat. But apparently the lesson I thought he'd learned the day before had leaked out of his forelock during the night. Although he didn't flee perhaps quite as far before I managed to wrestle him to a halt, he basically had the same reaction he'd had the first day.

So, sighing, I started anew. Robyn progressed a bit more quickly, and ended confidently, again. But, for several days and sessions, he tested my patience and skill. Each time he saw the mat, he'd gasp and snort, as if he'd never seen it before. He *was* able to progress more quickly each time. And, finally, the day came when the lesson seemed to take for real. I almost fell out of the saddle the first time Robyn calmly strode over the mat at the *beginning* of the lesson.

Robyn acted the same way with flags. Each time, after an extended session, I would convince him to calmly carry a rider with a flag. However, the next day, he'd start off like he'd never seen one before.

You may also have an animal that displays this learning cycle—taking three short steps forward, followed by two *long* ones back. Though some horses will retain the training from a single session and be ready to progress further, others will take longer. Have patience. Be persistent. Don't get frustrated.

CHAPTER 8

Bombproofing Skills Your Horse Should Possess

Every horse should be able to accomplish certain basic tasks, and that's what we're going to talk about in this chapter. Some of the tasks—riding in traffic, for instance—may seem less useful to you if you live on a farm, but it's always possible that you'll have to take your horse to a city or a suburb, and it would be nice not to worry that your horse is going to harm himself, someone else, or you. (I've included here the skills that seem the most applicable to my students in my clinics, and in many cases, given you pointers on where to find elaborate discussions of these concerns in earlier chapters.)

Cross Water and Other Obstacles

Whether it's a stream or a log, the bombproofing strategy is always the same. Use the skills that you developed in Chapter Seven to cross mattresses, tarps, and mats (p.103). First, *minimize the obstacle—* make it easy. It may be difficult to find an "easy" water obstacle, but you should look for a simple crossing with decent footing, a flat, shallow approach, and one that's wide enough so your horse can't jump it, but narrow enough not to be too daunting.

Next, get your horse to attempt the obstacle (in this case, the water) using all of the techniques I've discussed in Chapters Four, Five, and Seven. You can also use the *herd instinct* to help you. If he misbehaves, see *Dealing with Bad Habits and Nasty Tricks* (p. 89) for advice on how to thwart his behavior.

Then, through repetitions, build his confidence level. You may need to cross the water numerous times to accomplish this; further, you may need to repeat the lesson on subsequent days before he really absorbs it.

For further information, please note that this subject is covered extensively in Chapter Seven,

Bombproofing Day, and Chapter Five, *Working Your Horse from the Ground.*

Walk on Unusual Surfaces or Small Obstacles

The technique for walking on top of surfaces such as painted pavement is identical to that discussed above for crossing water and other obstacles.

Tolerate Loud Noises

This subject is covered extensively on page 135, *Firing Blanks.* The format of how to bombproof— that is, *minimize the obstacle, get your horse to attempt it,* then *build his confidence through repetitions*—is the same, even when you're getting your horse used to sounds. You use distance to *minimize this obstacle* by staying further away at first.

Deal with Unknown Odors

You can bombproof your horse to odors the same way you would bombproof him to anything else— the smell of flares and smoke, for example, are a very helpful way to accustom a horse to unexpected smells. Almost anything can be used to habituate your horse to unusual smells. Simply choose items that are outside the horse's habitual world—a desk chair, rubber tires, or a piece of carpeting.

The way to minimize this obstacle would be through distance. As he becomes accustomed to the strange smell, you can convince him to get closer. However, if you're out on the trail and simply have to try to get him by something that smells nasty, like a dead animal, use the active riding skills you learned in the Chapter Four.

Cope with Sudden Disturbances

This subject is partially covered in Chapter Six, *Dealing with Bad Habits and Nasty Tricks,* as well as

Chapter Seven, *Firing Blanks.* The problem with sudden disturbances is—well, that they're sudden! Since they're not predictable, it's impossible to prevent them, or your horse's reaction to them.

Try to develop a good, strong, seat so that you cannot be unseated by your horse in this kind of situation. His possible reactions may include spooking, wheeling, or bolting. Then, it becomes a matter of damage control. You simply have to try and get him back under control as quickly and effectively as possible (see Chapters Four, Five, and Six). Then, you have to try to take a deep breath and forget about it.

Self-Load into a Horse Trailer

Chapter Five, *Working Your Horse from the Ground,* taught you how to use a control halter. You're going to use that technique to help you here.

Self-loading simply means the horse willingly walks onto the trailer, on his own, *without* you walking in with him, and *without* your needing a second person to help you. As you probably know, walking in with your horse is dangerous: You risk him trying to back out before you can secure the rear bar.

Tying his head before you secure the rear bar can be dangerous if he starts pulling; if the halter or tie breaks, he may fly out of the back of the trailer. Also, if you always have to have at least two people to load your horse, you can't go places by yourself.

Here are some basic concepts to improve your horse's loading habits. Keep in mind that some of these techniques require a high degree of experience, so assess your own skill level before attempting them (photos 8.1 A to F).

I'm going to assume that you're using a two-horse trailer with a ramp, which is usually more difficult to load than a stock trailer.

1 If possible, begin the process by loading your horse with a calm, easy-to-load horse. Be sure that your horse is not afraid of the easy "loader."

2 Load the experienced horse first.

3 Now load the horse in training. Go ahead, lead him in, and have a second person secure the rear bar before you secure the horse's head. Also, make sure you are able to walk in without obstruction. The aisle should be clear and the chest bar should be open, as should the side door. *Do not try to duck under the chest bar!* If you do, you will have to hesitate and your body language may appear adverse to your horse. An open side door is more welcoming to the horse.

4 As you lead your horse on, be sure to throw the lead line over your horse's neck so neither of you steps on it. Do not throw it over at the last second, because your movement may startle him, and he may run away or evade because of your actions.

5 After you determine that he has done this procedure enough times to be totally at ease, test your horse: Load the experienced horse first, but this time, walk next to your horse and lead him to his side of the trailer. Walk straight ahead (not into the trailer), looking where you are going (not back at the horse), and direct the horse's head up the ramp and into the trailer.

Some technical notes here:
- This time the chest bar needs to be secured, because you don't want the horse to try and walk out the side door.
- Always lead your horse on the *outside*— meaning that if you're loading him on the left side, you walk on your horse's left side; and if loading him on the right, you walk on his right. In all likelihood, he'll evade by trying to step off the side of the ramp. If you are on the outside, you have a lot of advantages: you can more easily close the door, and you can help prevent a nasty injury by preventing your horse from sidestepping off the ramp and scraping his legs on the ramp itself.
- Be careful, of course, that the horse doesn't step on you!

6 Once he is in the trailer, immediately secure the rear bar. If you have a helper, she can go to your horse's head and hold him while you do this. Make sure your helper doesn't stick her head in the door to watch, which may distract your horse.

7 Your test may yield certain results:
- He may go straight in.
- He may stop partially in and hesitate, then go with a little encouragement from behind.

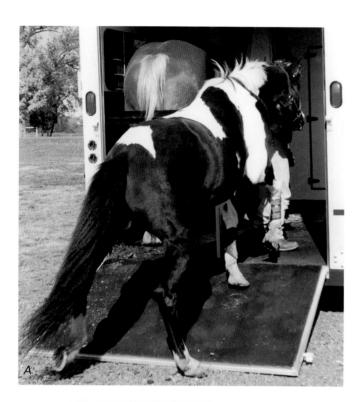

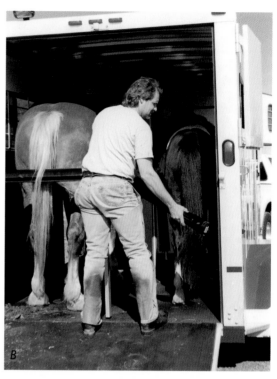

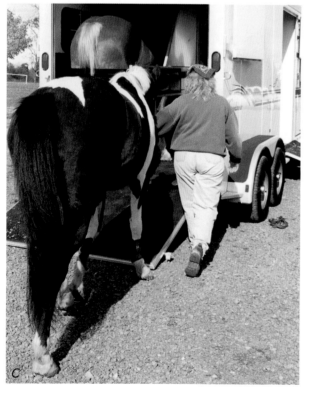

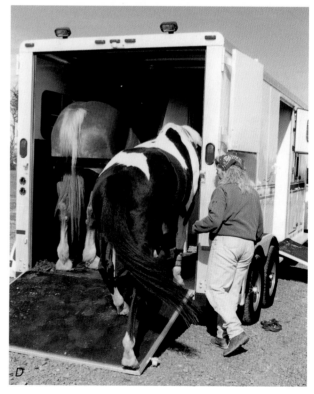

8.1 A—F
Trailer Loading

A. *After an experienced horse has been loaded and secured, lead the horse in training into the trailer.*

B. *As soon as the horse has walked on, have another person secure the hind bar while you tie the head.*

C. *Again, with the experienced horse loaded, lead your horse to the ramp and ask him to walk on by himself.*

D. *After the horse self-loads, be ready to secure the hind bar. If he should decide to back out of the trailer, you need to be ready to catch the lead line, which you will have draped over his neck. The chest bar must be secured to prevent him from trying to leave through the side door. After the horse has successfully self-loaded, close the hind bar, then move to his head to secure the halter tie.*

E. *Now, without the aid of the experienced horse, try leading your horse up to the ramp. You should ask him to walk up the ramp and onto the trailer by himself, as you did before.*

F. *Stay at the back of the trailer as the horse walks on, and be ready to catch his lead line should he back out. Once the horse has loaded himself, close the hind bar, and then secure his halter tie.*

- He may evade by stepping to the side.
- He may evade by totally stepping away from the ramp.
- He may stop before the ramp.
- He may go in and back out.

You need to have a response for each of these results, which I've listed from simple to most complex. Once again, your *timing* and *technique* are crucial. You will have to make an assessment quickly, and this is totally on instinct. Say the horse gets halfway in and stops. Do you let him take a moment to assess then continue on his own, or do you immediately tap his hind end to encourage him to get in? Either response may be appropriate. Some horses want to examine the trailer; others are looking for a way out and will take advantage of you, since you aren't behind him encouraging forward movement. (The latter horse will generally back out, by the way.) So you see, it depends on the horse and his motivation.

Your general response to evasions should be to close his options off, encourage forward movement, and do it in a timely manner. If you are too late in your response, he will already have evaded. If you are half-hearted in encouraging him forward, he won't listen to you.

8 Once he passes the test, again repeat this new loading procedure enough times so that he is loading in a relaxed, consistent manner. Once you feel he is comfortable, conduct another test: load him onto the trailer by himself, with no experienced horse to accompany him.

Since you're only loading one horse, close the rear bar of the empty side of the trailer. Use the left side, because that is the side you should always load a single horse on. (Note: It is the opposite in the UK and countries where you drive on the left side of the road.) Then, follow the techniques I discussed in Number 7. You might also consider using a chain across your horse's nose to discourage him from backing away and evading. Remember, this is the same concept as working the horse from the ground. It requires a higher level of skill, so only do it if you're comfortable. If not, find someone who is. If you do it wrong, you may cause more problems than you already had.

To add another tool to this technique, you should also carry a longe whip. This will enable you to encourage forward movement while walking straight ahead, since the whip is long enough to circle behind both you and your horse. Again, there is a higher degree of skill required here.

9 Finally, be sure to teach your horse to stand quietly in the trailer itself. Some horses believe that they have to get out of the trailer as soon as the truck stops. They start kicking, pawing, and otherwise being obnoxious until you let them out. If you rush in to get them out, you'll only be encouraging the horse to kick or paw the next time you stop. Your horse needs to get used to standing quietly in the trailer for reasonable amounts of time after it has stopped.

Again, it may be helpful to have an experienced horse standing quietly with your horse to ease his impatience and raise his comfort level. Whether or not you have another horse, simply force yourself to make your horse stand for longer and longer periods of time before you take him out of the trailer.

In general, these techniques have worked for me for over twenty years with very few problems. There are always exceptions, however. If you have a problem loader, you may want to get an experienced, qualified person to help you. Your technique and timing will be crucial, and it's difficult to learn this kind of technique and timing when you're working with a horse that already has a problem.

If the techniques I've provided don't work, first determine if your horse has had a bad experience—a trailer accident, for example. If that is the case, you have to proceed with much more encouragement and patience to reestablish trust of the trailer. If your horse hasn't had a bad experience, he simply may be obstinate. I remember two specific police horses that essentially did the same thing—as an officer walked the horses to the trailer, fully expecting the horses to walk on as they'd done countless times before, the horses would spin away at the last second. The officers often let go of the lead, and off the horses would gallop, saddles and all. It turned out that the horses only had this problem first thing in the morning when all their buddies were being turned out in the field. The problem horses were going to work while their friends had a day off. Once we determined the cause of the horses' resistance, it was easy to reschedule their trailer time. We also made it clear by using a chain across their noses that this type of behavior was *not* acceptable.

Keep in mind that once your horse gets away with something, he will try it again and again. It is extremely important to use that chain to discourage the horse from dangerous behavior. Extreme cases of resistance will require a high degree of skill using the chain and encouraging forward movement. The horse simply needs to understand that freedom and reward await him in the trailer.

Behave When Being Ridden in Company

Riding in Formations and Parades on page 157, includes a systematic approach to help you with this.

Deal with Strange Environments

Of course, it's up to you and your horse to determine if an environment is "strange." Horses used to outdoor arenas may panic or be uncomfortable in indoor arenas, for example—the question is whether the horse has had narrow or wide exposure to these kinds of situations. The more often you can teach your horse that the new training environments and obstacles are the norm, not the exception, the more your horse will adapt quickly to a different situation.

No matter what the situation, I generally use a three-step technique to adapt my horse quickly. First, I look for unsafe conditions—holes in the ground, low rafters, for example—that could cause injury to my horse, myself, or both of us. Second, I try to determine what specifically in the environment is bothering the horse. Is it the different lighting of an indoor arena? The way the sound echoes off the buildings? Third, and most importantly, I always have a plan to put my horse to work, to get his mind on something else. By now, you know what techniques work to make your horse bombproof—*leg-yielding*, for instance; putting him on the bit; or executing a half-halt. Whatever the technique, you want to use something that will make the horse focus on you and not what's troubling him. It may also help, of course, to use your horse's *herding instinct* and bring another, quiet animal in to accompany him.

Deal with Ground Distractions

In many cases, your horse will be distracted by objects he thinks he'll have to walk over, onto, or

8.2 A & B
The Slypner Shoe

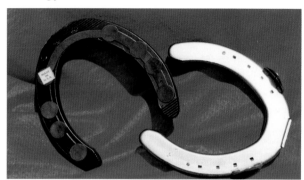

A. *Slypner shoes come in two pieces, a stainless-steel base that is nailed to the hoof, and a replaceable polyurethane insert that provides excellent traction and shock absorption on pavement and rough terrain.*

B. *An assembled Slypner shoe.*

near. Working your horse over mattresses, tarps, tires, and trash (see Chapter Seven) will be a big help. Of course, you should be riding proactively, looking for potential problems before they occur, but sometimes you'll require a bit more. Always keep in mind that a forward-moving horse is the goal, because a forward horse will be less likely to react adversely. Trotting past something is better than having the horse stop, whirl, and spin away. Don't forget that the horse has to stop and regroup in order to evade or flee.

To control shying, use the *head away* or *leg-yielding* exercises.

Riding in Traffic

Riding in a city, or even a suburb, comes with its own inherent set of difficulties. If you live in a populated area, your horse will have to learn to cope with traffic, noise, sirens, delivery trucks, construction, and people who are probably uneducated about horses. Even if you spend the majority of your time in a rural setting, you still may find yourself on a roadway at some point.

Of course, some people mount up in town due to their own, very unique circumstances. I recently read a bit of history about a song written by Allman Brothers guitarist Dickey Betts, called "Pony Boy." The song was about his uncle, who used to ride his horse to the local bar so he could drink and not worry about DWI charges.

If you're going to be riding on pavement for any length of time, you should consider having borium put on your horse's shoes, or consider using another type of shoe that will give you some traction. Pavement can be extremely slick. If your horse slips and falls on you, the consequences can be dire.

Rubber shoes work great on pavement, but are slippery on wet grass. I have found the Slypner shoes, which have a polyurethane insert in a stainless steel base, are quite effective on *both* grass and pavement. However, it's difficult to customize and mold them to fit oddly shaped hooves, because they fight to revert to their original shape (photos 8.2 A & B). (See the *Appendix* for suppliers.)

If you're riding in any kind of traffic, and you think your ride may stretch into the evening, you should get *reflectors* either to put on your horse's legs (typically, they're strapped onto the cannon-bone area), or to attach to your breastplate. If you decide to use leg reflectors, it's important that you apply them with even pressure and that they're not too tight (photo 8.3).

If you're wondering where to purchase such an odd product, various police supply companies on the Internet sell them (see *Appendix*, p. 175). And no, you *don't* need to be a police officer to place an order. Alternatively, you can use lights made for bicyclists that can be strapped on your arm, boot, or stirrup. These lights are battery operated and flash.

Usually, horses aren't too concerned with vehicles, because they have been habituated to them throughout their lives. Use the techniques discussed in Chapter Seven to accustom them to more unexpected vehicles—motorcycles and bicycles, for example. Most stables have tractors, trucks, and cars coming and going all the time, and many turnout fields are adjacent to the road. This, in effect, serves as a type of real-life bombproofing for horses, accomplished by constant repetition in their environment.

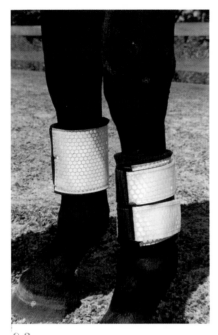

8.3

Leg Reflectors

Reflective equipment is a good idea for any kind of twilight or night riding. This is an example of a leg reflector.

When riding in the street, normally you should ride with traffic, instead of against it, because horses are more intimidated by things coming at them. Therefore, vehicles approaching from the rear are less likely to spook your horse. However, sometimes these vehicles get pretty close. To increase your safety, remember to use the *head away* exercise.

Since your horse is probably not concerned about the vehicles whizzing by on his left, he'll be inclined to shy or jump into the traffic if something "truly frightening" appears on his right. (It's the opposite in the UK.) Obviously—at least obviously to *you*—the real danger is the traffic. Photos 8.4 A to D show how we habituated one horse to the terrors of an umbrella while a car was nearby. In the first photograph, the horse has spooked from the umbrella. In the next two photos, the rider performed a *head away*, keeping his distance from both the vehicle and the umbrella. In the final picture, the *head away* has helped the horse successfully negotiate the way between umbrella and car.

Remember the mechanics of how a horse spooks. When he shies from an object on the right, he turns to look at the thing that scared him. Simultaneously, his hind end will swing the other direction. Use of the *head away* exercise will position your horse's hind end toward the curb and his head toward the traffic. Consequently, he'll be able to see

8.4 A—D
Traffic Concerns

A. *When something, in this case an umbrella, spooks a horse, the horse tends to spin. The real problem here, however, is the car coming down the road—and there is concern that the horse will jump out in front of the car trying to get away from the umbrella.*

B. *After regaining control of her horse, the rider executes the head away. In this position, not only can the horse see the approaching car, but his head is turned away from the umbrella. If the horse does not shy again, he is at a safer angle to the car: an angle that will help prevent his hind end from swinging into the street.*

C. *As the horse gets closer to the umbrella, he raises his head as he becomes more frightened. Because the rider remembers to keep the horse moving forward and maintains the head away, she keeps control.*

D. *The rider's proactive riding skills enable her to prevent the horse from spinning to the right, and they both pass the umbrella safely.*

the traffic, and additionally, you'll have a jump on thwarting any attempt he makes at shying.

Of course, you won't ride like this all the time, with your horse cranked sideways. Use the *head away*, and the other exercises you learned in Chapter Two, *Basic Training Exercises*, as needed.

Alleys

Even though alleys are just streets, since they're closed in on both sides and narrow, horses often find them scary. Your horse's prey-animal instincts tell him that it's easy to get trapped in a confined area. Added to that, alleys are usually bustling with activity, often on both sides. Keeping your horse forward will help to prevent him from balking and resisting.

Pedestrians

Riding in an urban environment means that you need to be very aware of your surroundings. Try to anticipate problems. One of your biggest difficulties may be pedestrians. You may be doing nothing more chancy than standing still quietly, but if a small child approaches suddenly from the rear or side, dire circumstances can result. If your horse is startled, he may easily step on the child. Particularly when youngsters are present, you need to keep your eyes open, because children are not as aware of danger as an adult might be. Not that adults are necessarily blessed with horse sense—you need to keep your eyes on them, as well. If I know that I will be standing somewhere for a period of time, I try to position my horse with a wall, tree, or some object behind him. That will eliminate *one* approach route for humans.

If someone wants to touch your horse, have him stand in front of where your leg lies on your horse so you can watch him, but don't let him stand directly in front of you. A toddler standing beneath your horse's chest can be trampled, or stick his fingers in your horse's mouth. The best strategy is to keep people to one side, and let them stroke your horse's neck or shoulder. Even then, make sure everyone's feet are not too close to your horse's hooves. Simply by stomping at a fly, your horse can squish a kid's foot.

People also may unwittingly frighten your horse. Invariably, someone with a child in a stroller will wheel it at your horse. It takes a stouthearted beast to stand his ground with one of these horrors coming at him. The dilemma is complicated further when the person keeps coming at your horse, not understanding that *they* may be causing the problem.

Windows, Curbs, Grates

Plate glass windows on stores can be lethal if your horse backs into them. Position him so he can't. Also notice where the curbs are located. They may trip your horse and cause him to fall backward if they're behind him. And while steel grates in the street *should* support you and your horse's weight, you shouldn't chance it. Stay off them.

Road Surfaces

Road or sidewalk surfaces vary in their degree of slipperiness. You can't always tell by their appearance, either. A resurfacing product has been applied to some of the bike paths in my area that's extremely slippery to shod horses, even those with borium-enhanced shoes. It looks just like regular asphalt. Turning, moving downhill, or speed will accentuate this slick tendency. Keep this in mind, and use extra caution. If you end up on a surface that feels like ice under your horse's feet, get *off* it.

You can't always safely perform training exercises when you're out in the real world. A busy street isn't the place to habituate your horse to *anything*.

Besides risking your own skull, you need to consider the safety of pedestrians and those riding in cars. Instead of thinking about bombproofing your horse, think about simply *managing* him.

An acceptable training situation needs to be free from traffic or other dangerous circumstances. I'll give you an example of such an situation. Once I was hacking on an empty bike path. Off to one side, a man was using a leaf blower. My mount became very tense. I was beginning to look for an escape route when the guy noticed me and turned off the leaf blower. However, it didn't help. My horse was already convinced the man was dangerous. I took the widest route possible (to increase my horse's *comfort zone*), used *head away*, and a few taps from my whip to convince my horse to proceed. Sure enough, the combined effects worked.

Since nobody was there for my mount to trample, I asked the guy if he could help me. He happily agreed and asked what he could do. Initially, I requested that he simply stand and hold the dreaded blower. I hacked my horse back and forth by him repeatedly, getting progressively closer. Then, I had him start the leaf blower and continued the exercise until we were standing quietly next to it.

CHAPTER 9

Formation Riding and Parades

FORMATION RIDING

Here's another way your group can work together to perfect your skills and those of your horses while having *fun*.

Participating in a parade, or just riding in formation, presents the opportunity to further instill obedience and confidence in your horse. Many horses object to riding in formation at first. Your mount may not *like* other horses close to him. He may be afraid of being kicked, or being bumped. Conversely, he might decide to plow into the rest of the pack, to tread on their tails, and sniff their manes. Your horse might canter in place, thinking he is about to race the other horses. His entire focus may be on how to *win* the exciting, new competition.

Through parade schooling, your horse will reach the point where he can move calmly, in unison with the other horses in the group. Then you'll have progressed further toward making him a well-behaved, reliable, user-friendly animal.

In addition, these activities will build your own accuracy and proficiency, because to keep up with your group, you need to anticipate your mount's reactions. To halt, or trot, or turn, when so ordered, *instead* of when you think the moment is right, will demand that you keep your aids on and your wits sharp.

To teach you how to ride in organized formation, as you would want to in a parade, I'll use eight horses as an example. I'll present some basic patterns that you and your friends can practice. Ideally, you have a number in your group that's divisible by four, so your movements appear even. However, you have to adjust accordingly for the number of horses and riders. If you have nine horses in your group, your solution will be more complex than simply splitting into groups of three. The difficulty with an odd number of riders is that moving from groups of three to two, and then back again, is *awkward*. Certainly, if your gathering of friends includes nine, you don't have to vote out the most unpopular member. Just know that if you are trying to impress someone with your group's ability to change formations, the plan probably won't work. Once I explain the movements, you'll see why, and you'll *definitely* figure it out once you've tried them. I've included suggestions about various ways to surmount some of the difficulties presented by an odd number of riders later in this chapter.

The leading file rider was called a *guide on* in the cavalry. The *guide on* would carry a flag that could be seen by the rest of the troops to better maintain *dress* (*dress* means how everyone lines up with each other, see p.162) and anticipate troop movement.

Though you can call her whatever you like, you need to pick a leader who'll give the commands and travel in front of the rest of the group. Make sure you choose someone who knows how to shout commands, and isn't shy or impatient. Make sure to choose a person who everyone in the group respects, as well. Your group will get confused if riders other than the leader interfere and attempt to take over commands.

Because your leader is in the front, in order to be heard, she'll have to turn around to give commands. When she does this, it will be a two-part process. First, she needs to say what she wants your group to do. This is the *preparatory command*. A *preparatory command* means just that. Its purpose is to warn the riders that they will soon be asked to execute that movement. If your leader says "Halt," that means all the riders in your group should prepare to do so, but none of you should *actually* halt, until the *execution command* is given. Without the *preparatory command*, it would be impossible for the riders to perform movements simultaneously.

The *execution command* will shortly follow the *preparatory command*. In our police department, we use the word "Whoa," and that's what you should use as well. Therefore, to put your group in motion, your leader will say "Forward." At that juncture, the riders in your group should gather up their reins, and prepare to walk. Shortly thereafter, your leader will say "Whoa," and immediately, all of the riders in your group should push their horses into a walk.

Once your group hears "Whoa"—the *execution command*—you should all scramble to perform the movement *immediately*. Otherwise, your formation will begin to look like a freight train. A freight train starts moving in the front. Then, one by one, the rest of the cars down the line squeak into motion. Obviously, this *isn't* the desired effect. Everyone needs to ask his or her horse to perform at the same time. Forget the notion that the person in front of you has to move first. As soon as you hear the "Whoa" command, execute the movement that was called for. Even if you are running into the rear of the horse in front of you, trot when it is demanded.

Your buddies will get the hint with practice. If they don't, remind them to move out at the same moment as you do. This is important advice to follow when performing any of the commands. All the riders should move together, as a unit, to lend your group a polished, impressive look. Timing is *everything*.

For clarity's sake, your leader should use the same commands each time for the same movement. For example, if she wants you to move into a single-file line, she should always say, "Column of one," for the *preparatory command*. If she sometimes says that, and sometimes says "Single file," or "On your own, now, baby," it's more difficult for the riders to understand, particularly if conditions make it tough to hear. Our department has found the phrases, "Column of one, Column of twos," etcetera, as simple as any.

9.1
Single File into Pairs

Start with a straight line of horses. The even-numbered horses are moved out, and now ride next to the odd-numbered horses. The result is pairs of horses, riding in two lines.

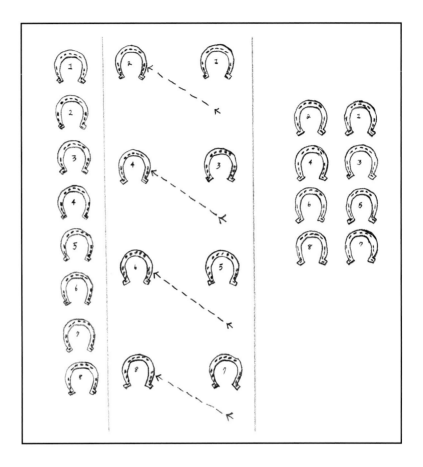

Unless told otherwise, work at the walk. Stay at that gait until your leader tells you to trot, canter, or halt. In fact, stay at *whatever* gait directed, until you receive a command to change it. Therefore, if you're trotting, and a command is called to pair up or turn, you shouldn't stop. You pair up or turn *while* trotting.

Changing from one formation to another will necessitate that some riders will have to increase their speed, or decrease it, in order to close up the gaps. When done correctly, the riders in front will maintain a steady pace. It's the job of those following to adjust.

Starting in Single File

To start, your leader can move to the front of your formation. Advantages *do* exist by placing the leader in other spots, such as out to the side or at the rear. For example, with the leader in the rear, it's easier for her to shout commands. However, you can experiment with these different positions later.

Your group will start by putting your horses in a straight line, head to tail. The ideal distance between your horses is four feet, at least, to start with. After you gauge your horses' reactions, making sure the mount in the lead isn't considering kicking the one behind him, you want to tighten up your formation. Ideally, the distance you want to strive to achieve is a mere one-foot apart in single file. However, the more horses abreast, the more distance you need to maintain from nose to tail. When traveling in pairs, you need to be three feet apart, and when traveling in fours, the distance will stretch even further, to about eight feet apart. From the start, you want to practice keeping your distances exact, so that your formation will look smart.

You also need to try to stay in a straight line with one another. When viewed from the front or rear, your column should be so aligned that a person viewing it sees only the first or last rider. If your line isn't straight, it will be obvious. Those out of line will be sticking out to one side or another.

The next step is for you to "number off." The easiest way to accomplish this is to have the first rider holler "one," over his shoulder, the second "two," and so on, until all of you have been assigned numbers, from one to eight. Remember your number.

Moving from Single File into Pairs

The first actual movement I'll explain to you is how to expand the single-file line you've formed into pairs. When your leader has given both the *preparatory* "Column-of-twos" *command*, and the *execution command* "Whoa," the even-numbered riders in your group should ride up and next to the left side of the odd-numbered riders. The rule to remember is this: the line *looms* to the left and *reduces* to the right. For example, to move into pairs, the number two rider travels up to the left side of number one, the number four rider to the left of number three, and so on (fig. 9.1).

Once this is accomplished and the horses in your group have paired up, everybody will have to close up the gaps abandoned by the even horses.

All of the pairs, save the one leading your pack, will have to increase their pace. The leading pair maintains the original pace. To help maintain a crisp formation, try to imagine that you're attached to your partner.

Problems Already?

This early section of this chapter is devoted to explaining the mechanics of how to ride in formation, and, for clarity's sake, I'm going to continue as if all of your horses are perfectly accepting of your new plans. However, we all know that life with horses is rarely this simple. If you have problems with your horse—kicking, biting, having a nervous breakdown when forced to take the rear— skip to the section later in this chapter, *Troubleshooting* (p. 166).

Moving Back to Single File from Pairs

To change *back* from the pairs formation into a single-file column again, the reverse will happen. The even-numbers will hold back and fade to the right to align themselves with the hind ends of the odd-numbered horses. The number two horse will wait and move to the right, to adjust herself in line with the bottom of the number one horse. The number four horse will similarly be asked to scoot behind number three (fig. 9.2).

The same basic premises hold true for moving into, and back from, columns of four, or even eight. To move into columns of four from columns of two, follow the same procedures you used to pair up. The even pairs move to the left of the odd pairs. Therefore, the pair made up of the number four and number three horse hurry forward, and to the left, until they are even with the pair made up of the number two and number one horse.

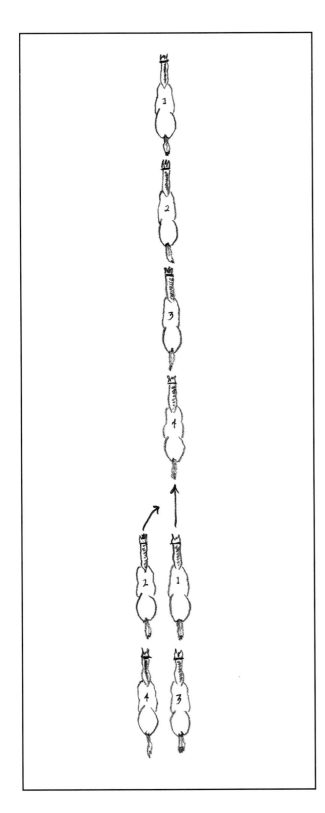

To ride from pairs back into singles: The even-numbered horses fall in behind the horse on their right (the odd-numbered horses), resulting in a single line—odd, even, odd, even, and so forth.

Your group should also practice moving from single file to a column of fours. When moving into larger sections, it's important for the even-numbered riders to move out quickly, trotting if necessary. They have to increase their speed, while those assigned odd numbers maintain the pace originally set.

The next, and final expansion is to move into a column of eights. It's done the same way as in the previous examples, but since the lines are larger, it gets more challenging. Your group needs to pay attention to keep proper spacing, distance, and move in accord with each other. Also, the rider on the far left must make sure that she allows enough distance, so as to not close or pinch the riders to her right.

Turns

Your group will want to practice the following types of turns. Don't worry—these movements sound far more complex than they are. It may help you to glance at the diagrams included in this chapter to better understand who goes *where*.

9.3
90-Degree Turn

To perform a 90-degree turn, the horses on the inside track move more slowly than those on the outside track. Remember to "dress" right—the horse on the outside track sets the pace while the horses on the inside track keep up. Keep equal distance between horses side-to-side and front-to-back.

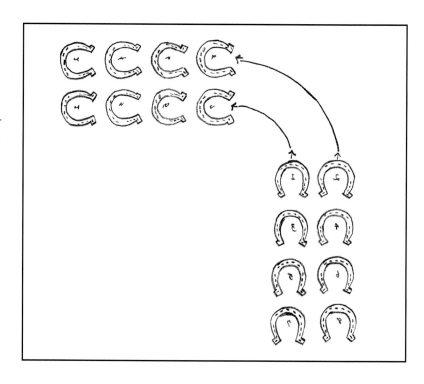

90-Degree Turn

When the command, "Column left" (or right), is given, your unit should perform a 90-degree turn, or a turn that if, from viewed from above, would describe a quarter of a circle. A "Column half left" means your group should perform a 45-degree turn (one-eighth of a circle). Obviously, in this case, your turn would be to the left. From here on, I'll consider the direction self-explanatory (fig. 9.3).

"U"-Turn

When you hear, "Column about," it refers to a complete U turn: one-half circle, or a hundred-and-eighty degrees (fig. 9.4).

The Wheel

The Wheel is the same as a turn, but with one very distinct difference. A wheel actually pivots on the inside rider, whereas in a turn, the inside rider should be riding a small arc. This command should be used for more than two horses. Wheels come in the same variations as column turns. That is, wheel left (or right), wheel half left (or right), and wheel about left (or right). (See fig. 9.5).

Dress

To appear polished and professional, your group will need to perfect their *dress*. As I mentioned earlier, this word is a fancy term that refers to being correctly positioned in relation to the other riders. You are properly *dressed* when you're lined up straight with them, both from front-to-back and side-to-side.

Front-to-Back Dress

You already know how to maintain front-to-back *dress*. The person in front of you is the one that determines how fast you go. She's the one you *dress* on. Just line-up directly behind her. You need to

9.4
U-Turn

To perform the U-Turn, the front horse on the outside track (marked "X") will set the pace, since he will have a longer distance to cover than those on the inside tracks. "Dress" right—inside tracks watch the outside track horses and keep up with them. Try to keep equal distance side-to-side and front-to-back. After the turn has been made, continue in straight lines.

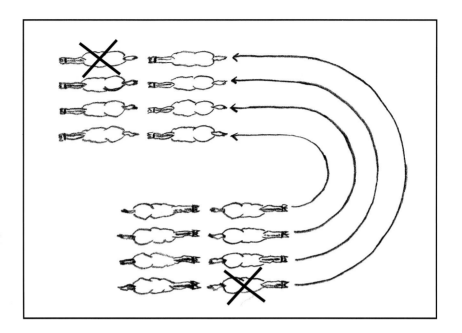

9.5
The Wheel

To perform the Wheel, the horse on the outside track, (marked "X"), will set the pace as this horse has the most distance to travel. When the lines are very long, the outside-track horse may be cantering, while the inside-track horse is walking. "Dress" right—watch the speed of the outside track horse. Keep the line straight side-to-side. Once the turn has been completed, continue in a straight line in the new direction.

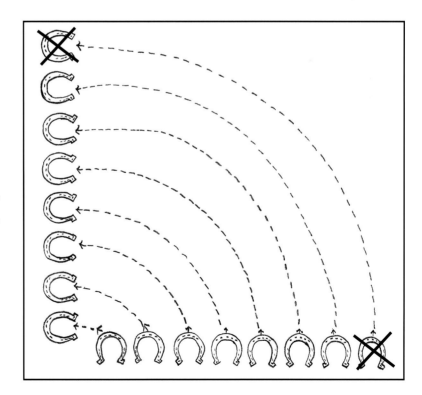

insure your horse is straight, as well, without his hindquarters popped to the side. From side-to-side, you eventually want your boots to almost touch those of the rider next to you, so the riders in front will have to pay extra close attention, since their positioning will ultimately determine the positioning of the rest of the group.

Side-to-Side Dress

Side-to-side *dress* is established by lining up with each other's shoulders. It's a mistake to try to line-up on the head of your partner's horse—or his shoulders, or withers—because each horse is unique in his length. However, if your shoulders are *dressed* (or *positioned* next to each other), your line will look straight. This right-to-left, side-to-side *dress* is the hardest to maintain.

Of course, *one* of the riders in each column you form will need to determine the pace. Each rider needs to be able to check her position at a glance and determine if she's correct or not. Normally, you check your side-to-side position by focusing on the rider on the far right of the column. *She's* the one that you need to line-up with. Just remember the "rider-on-right-rule."

There *is* one exception to this last rule. When making a turn, always *dress* to the outside of the turn. The reason for this is that when turning, the outside horse has to travel faster than the inside horse. And the effect grows with the column. The longer it is, the faster the outside rider will have to go. When a column of eight wheels around, the inside person will barely be squeaking along in a walk. The person at the *outside* of the turn is probably trotting vigorously, or even cantering. Since the turn is hardest on her, she gets to set the pace.

Besides making sure that her pace is aiding the effort to *dress*, it's the responsibility of the outside rider to make a proper turn. She needs to be careful to not cut it short and pinch the line. It's also her job to look ahead to determine the direction your unit travels.

Dressing on the outside person (on a turn) may take a bit of getting used to, since when turning left, the riders in your group (except for the outside one) will need to look *right*, instead of only where they're going.

How to Do These Movements with an Odd Number

Although, for simplicity's sake, I've used a group of eight horses as an example, you may well have an odd number, instead. If your unit contains eleven, don't despair. Here's how you can position yourselves. A group of eleven should divide into two columns of four, and one column of three. The column of three will bring up the rear. You can concoct a similar formation for seven horses, or for nine. In the last column, just leave an empty spot, as if there were a fourth in the group. To *see* what your columns should look like, see Figure 9.6.

You can also solve the odd-number problem by having one person riding by himself in the back. Conversely, your leader can ride in front of your unit, out of formation. This can appear dramatic, particularly if he's carrying a flag.

As usual, your columns will *dress* to the right. Remember, this means that all of you will line-up on the rider *to* your right.

If you want to have three groups of three for a parade, so you look uniform, that's fine, of course. However, *forget* changing formations as you've learned. It *is* possible to change the number in your columns by first getting in a single-file line, then moving into pairs. To reverse the process, return to single-file columns first, and then back to columns of threes.

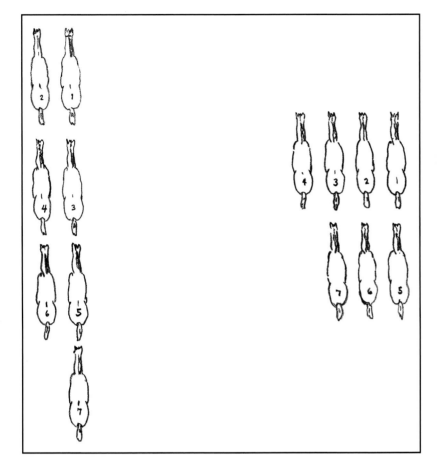

9.6
The Missing Horse

When formation work with an odd number of horses is performed, the "missing horse" is ignored. Columns of singles-to-doubles are performed in the same manner as they are when there is an even number of horses, except the last horse rides alone.

You may find it necessary, when riding in a noisy environment, to pass commands down the line. If you find your group can't hear your leader, you can try this method. All it requires is some patience. Each rider hollers over his shoulder to "pass" the *preparatory command* to the next. As soon as the *preparatory command* has been passed to all of the riders, all of you need to listen and watch carefully. The next command will obviously be the *execution* one, so it doesn't matter if you can hear *it* exactly or not. You'll know, as soon you see your leader gesture, what she's saying.

If you prefer, you can use some simple hand signals instead. If it's decided to use signals, these are the ones your leader should use, as they are the easiest to understand:

Your leader should hold up her index finger when she wants you to move into a column. She should hold up two fingers for columns of two, and four fingers for columns of four. When she raises her fist, this will mean she wants your group to slow to the next slowest gait. If your group is already walking, her raised fist means she wants you to halt. If her fist pumps up and down, she wants you to increase your speed to the next gait. As the hand signal tells you your leader's intent, *it* is the *preparatory command*. The signal for execution is when her hand falls suddenly forward.

This technique produces much more polished results with practice, so if you think you may need to use it, your group will want to practice *before* the event.

Troubleshooting—Dealing with Common Horse Problems

Although you now understand the basics of how you should ride in formation, the problem remains of getting your mounts to comply. This type of riding tends to bring up some fairly typical dilemmas with horses. Here's how to surmount them.

Trotting in Place

If your horse canters or trots in place, he's probably worried that the others are leaving him. He may well work himself into a lather, overwhelmed by the idea that the herd is going to outpace him. The way to fix this is to initially put him in the front. Once he's settled down, you can gradually begin moving him back in the formation. Over time, you'll be able to place him anywhere in the line. You'll need patience, persistence, repetition, and positive reinforcement to teach your horse—the same as you would when teaching any other bombproofing skill.

Your Horse Is Scared of Other Horses

If your horse gets upset when the others are too close, it may be because he dislikes (or is afraid of) a specific animal. If a nasty mare with a big bottom pins her ears and gives your horse the evil eye whenever he closes the distance, you may never be able to change his mind about her. If so, just ride next to another horse.

More likely, though, it's just a matter of getting your mount used to a new experience. To build his confidence, simply ride at a comfortable distance from the other horses. Remember how you minimized the intensity of various problems using distance in your bombproofing work? This works on the same principle. Gradually, as your horse relaxes, close the gap until he's in line with the rest of the horses. Besides your usual patience and persistence, you also need the cooperation of your friends. Hopefully, you'll have understanding buddies who'll help you solve this problem.

Your Horse Wants to Attack Other Horses

The dilemma is a slightly different one if *your* horse is the nasty one who tries to bite and kick the others. This is obviously *not* a good way to cement a friendship. It may be, again, that your mount has a problem with a specific animal. As in the previous situation, if this is the case, the easiest solution is simply to separate the two enemies.

However, aggression is a different sort of disobedience than fear. You have greater control over belligerent misbehavior. Your horse needs to be punished for merely *thinking* about biting or kicking. Otherwise, you are risking injury to your friends and their horses. Remember, since you're striving to ride boot-to-boot, the distance between horses is pretty close. You need to pay close attention to your horse's body language. If his ears are flattened against his head, or he snakes his neck in the other horse's direction, this should clue you in to his ill intentions. You should be able to detect his slightest "dirty look." Also, watch and feel for kicking intent—for your mount's hind end moving over or tensing.

To correct this kind of ugly behavior, you need to have enough contact with your horse's mouth to reprimand him immediately. Straighten his neck and bump the reins if he glances at the other horse in an unfriendly manner. Your heel can give him a nudge, too. He needs to understand that he'll be punished for his behavior. If your horse's bottom is sidling

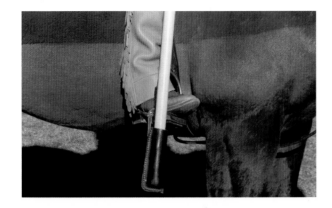

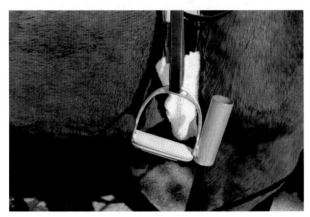

9.7 A & B
Flag Holder

Examples of two types of flag holders. One attaches to the stirrup and is made of thick leather. The other, a metal type, is soldered onto the stirrup.

toward another horse, use your leg, crop, and rein to scoot in the opposite direction. Supplement your correction with the voice command "Quit!"

RIDING IN PARADES

So, you've spent time doing a little formation training. Your group can keep a straight line, and further, has trained with flags. Now, you're ready to take the plunge and ride in the parade itself. Let's talk about what that involves, from initially

filling out the registration forms, to the conclusion, when your group arrives back at the trailers.

Necessary Equipment

You will need a flag holder if you'll be carrying a flag for any length of time. Flag holders that attach to your stirrup are free to move around a little, and are a bit more comfortable than—and don't give as much as—the stirrups that have a piece of metal welded directly onto them (photos 9.7 A & B). If you carry a flag for any length of time, your knee will end up taking the torque. After a couple of hours, this subtle movement will become *much* more obvious.

If you are going to be carrying a flag, you'll find it much easier to control your horse if you knot the reins over the withers (photo 9.8).

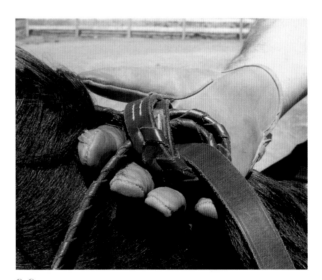

9.8
Knot the Reins

Knotting your reins allows you to ride with one hand when you need to free up the other. This technique can be used for riders carrying flags.

A consistent theme will add a polished look to your group. If you're a club, it's fun to get *matching shirts or jackets*. You can also order *saddle pads with your logo* on them. Further, *matching boots* for the horses can make them look more alike and spiff things up. And you may want to get a *flag made with your club logo*.

Preparation
Registering in the Parade

Most parades require you to fill out a registration or an application form. While the majority of these forms are pretty self-explanatory, sometimes "animal unit" or "horsed unit" aren't included in their list of categories. If this is the case, call parade officials to help place you in the appropriate group. Usually, parades give awards for categories.

Try to get your lineup position as soon as possible. You should also ask for a realistic "step off" time. Sometimes, the parade starts at nine in the morning, but officials often ask you to be there as early as seven. However, if your group is positioned in the middle of a large parade, you might not step off until eleven. Obviously, that's a lot of standing around—especially on a hot day. If they absolutely *demand* that you're there early, send a representative to take care of any details required. Then, your group can show up at a reasonable time, and avoid a lot of waiting.

Ask About Cleanup

Sometimes, the parade will provide cleanup service. However, other times the officials will ask you to provide a warm body to help. Hopefully, one of your club members will be able to coerce his or her spouse to do the duty. Of course, the abused spouse should be provided with a vehicle to make the job easier.

Your group might also consider volunteering to provide cleanup in exchange for a better parade position. Many times the parade organizers move the horses further back in the order because someone complains that they don't want to be behind them and their inherent messes. If you find out that's why you're being shuffled to the back, then offer cleanup.

Arrange Friends to Help

You should always bring a friend to provide support on foot. Your friend can assist in many ways. She can arrive at the parade's start position and check in your unit. She can verify your position and staging area for your lineup. If one of your members needs to hand off a flag, drops something, or needs tack adjusted, she can solve the problem. Further, in the parade itself, she can stroll behind your group, and keep the following unit at a comfortable distance.

This duty will become especially important if the group behind yours is a band or a club with flags and pompons. Many times, people who don't deal with horses on an everyday basis will traipse right up to their rear ends. This is often true even when your horses are spinning around and dancing in place.

Ideally, the parade organizers will allow your ground helper to drive a vehicle behind your group. Then she can carry supplies—like raincoats, on those questionable days. If they do allow you this luxury, you'll need to find two friends. One can drive, and the other can climb out of the car when needed.

Trailer Parking

Find out about trailer parking. Try to arrange for a place at the end of the route with the parade organizers. That way, at the conclusion, your group can simply ride over to your trailers and leave.

Officials might have other ideas. They may well have parking in a particular place for specific reasons. If the parking place isn't suitable, explain the problems to them. They may not have thought about logistical issues with horses, and may have you parking right next to the band. That makes for a bad situation when you're trying to get tacked-up, dressed, and do last minute cleanup, no matter *how* schooled your horses are. Minimize unnecessary distractions.

Another option is to examine the parade route ahead of time and arrange your own parking. Shopping center lots work well. If you use one, park as far away from the stores as possible. Remember to get permission *before the day* from the store manager. Assure him you'll clean up any mess left. Parades are community events, and horses are popular, so garnering permission may be easier than you imagine.

You can also park in public lots, but make sure that you have room to get out when the time comes to leave. People coming to watch the parade have to park somewhere, and if space is scarce, they may forget their manners. *Anticipate* that someone will park a car in your way. If you park across spaces, you should angle your truck so you can drive right out. You may even want to invest in some traffic cones to keep other vehicles from parking too close. The average driver may park without regard to the fact that you need room to load your horse, and will need even more to maneuver the truck and trailer out of the lot.

If you do have to ride back to the beginning of the parade to return to your trailers, you may have to find an alternate route. The route you rode in on may still be blocked with the parade.

Consider How You'll Place Your Horses

You should consider the placement of your horses. The horses on each end will be subjected to the most stimulation. Therefore, the mounts positioned there should be the ones *least* likely to suffer meltdowns. The more fragile creatures should be sandwiched somewhere between the two ends. If one of your group is riding a horse that you think may need to turn around, place him second in from an end. That way, the disruption he causes won't be as noticeable. If he's in the middle, he'll succeed in interfering with the whole line.

The Actual Event
Getting Tacked-Up

Tacking-up at a parade can present difficulties. The Boy Scout troops, cheerleaders, and floats can be quite overwhelming. When your horse breaks free and runs screaming through the middle of the Elk's Club group, things tend to get even *more* exciting.

To avoid this kind of undesirable adrenaline boost, I like to trailer the horses partially tacked, with their saddles on. I leave the bridles off until I'm ready to unload. However, to be on the safe side, when I *do* put them on, it's while the horses are still trapped in the trailer. I recommend that you do the same with your horses.

If you try and bridle your horse once he's been unloaded, you may have to contend with him looking around and stepping on your toes while you struggle with his throatlatch. If he becomes frightened at a critical moment, you'll have a loose horse. Bridling in the trailer minimizes the chance of this.

Many people believe trailering saddled horses is dangerous. However, mounted police almost always transport their horses this way. For us, it's necessary.

When working, throughout the day, we may load and unload our horses several times. Personally, I've never had, or seen, problems result from the practice. Of course, the stirrups are run up first, to reduce the risk of them catching on something, and our girths aren't hanging loose. I have seen broken bridles, though—so we don't transport with them on, unless it's an emergency.

Riding to the Staging Area

When you ride to the staging area, look professional. I suggest you ride in columns of two. If you come to a narrow passage, your leader can signal your unit to go to single file until there's adequate room to return to pairs.

Once you've arrived at the staging area, line-up, if possible. If there's not room, find a place from which your group can easily fall into place as the parade passes. This is another instance where having a friend on foot can be a great aid. She can help coordinate getting your group into line as the parade starts. As always, try to stay away from the bands.

Your Formation and Possible Mutiny

As the parade starts, get into your formation. Straight lines are the easiest to maintain and look the best. Don't forget to watch your *dress. Dress,* as always, on the far right person, your leader. Besides determining your speed, he should be the one to make decisions.

Even if the situation gets stressful, remember to listen to him. This is easy in the police department, because it's habit. However, sometimes civilians mutiny under pressure. The worst thing that can happen is if your leader and another rider from your group start vying for command. A parade is no time to quarrel. If you get into problem circumstances, let your leader make the decision. You can critique him later.

Keeping the Pace

As you ride the parade route, you'll probably find that the pace isn't ideal for horses. To keep your distance from the unit in front of you—something you have to do—you need to be patient. Usually, the parade's speed will be slower than your mount's walk. Because of this, you'll be constantly stopping and then pressing into motion again.

Try to creep along as slowly as possible, so you don't have to stop. Moving forward is a good way to keep your horses occupied. Unfortunately, no matter how much you try to slow, staying in motion may be almost impossible. However, a horse that's manageable while moving may become extremely unhappy while halted. This is particularly true when activity is buzzing behind him—a pretty typical situation in a parade!

Most of the time your horse only wants to look at what is behind him. Although it may not look great to have him turned the wrong way, I suggest you permit him to take a peek, anyhow. You may even find it necessary to let your horse stand facing the opposite way from the other horses. While getting a look at "the monster" may ease your horse's concern, only allow this concession when you stop.

If You Plan to Carry Flags

If you carry flags, you should know the proper placement for protocol. The leading horse, on the far right, will carry the Stars and Stripes. If not placed there, it should be carried to the front and center, by itself. It should also be the tallest flag. More than the pole will determine the height that it reaches. It's also affected by the height of the horse, as well as the rider's stirrup length, since that's where the carrier is attached. A tall rider on a tall horse with a long leg may actually cause the flag to be too *low.*

Dipping the flags means to put your arm out straight. This action will put the flags at an angle. The reason you dip the other flags is to honor the American one.

When you dip a flag, it's a good idea to hold it against the pole. A dipped flag will tend to drop down near, or sometimes even in front of, your horse's face, and this can cause him to stop, whirl, or back-up. You might want to take this precaution even if you *have* worked to condition your horse to the flag. While preparing him with training sessions *should* help, it always seems that the actual event can bring out a horse's worst behavior.

The wind is another factor to consider. If you have a horse getting out of hand because the flags are blowing, you may have to hold the flag during the parade. It looks much better if they're flying, but you have to weigh the benefits against the reaction of the horses. You *won't* look good if your horses are flying faster than the flags.

Moving from right to left (from the riders perspective), after the American flag, the flags should be carried in the order of state, then county, then unit. When you pass the parade review stand, it's customary to dip all the flags—except for the American flag. It remains straight and tall. Of course, other countries have their own rules to follow.

Your Bombproofed Horse

If you've got this far, you're either cheating and reading the end first, or you've worked with your horse through a wide variety of obstacles, issues, and problems. Keep in mind that no horse is ever fully, totally, and completely bombproof—there may always be something that you can't get him used to; there may be new situations or problems that come up; and of course it's impossible to always expect the unexpected. But, your horse's confidence should have increased dramatically.

Confidence isn't something that will appear overnight. But, as you work your horse through more and more situations, you'll find that it will build—and your own confidence will build exponentially, too. Unexpected and difficult objects will seem less unexpected and less difficult—to both of you. Challenges that once seemed impossible—and completely intimidating—can be passed and surpassed. No matter what riding discipline, no matter your experience level, no matter what kind of horse you're paired with, your new confidence should make *all* of your daily equestrian activities more enjoyable. And that's the point, isn't it? To have fun!

APPENDIX

Resources

Cage Balls

Olympia Sports
www.olympiasports.com
(800) 521-2832

Buy Sports Equipment
www.buy-sports-equipment.com
(414) 425-8575

Shape Up Shop
www.shapeupshop.com

Dually Schooling Halter™

Monty & Pat Roberts, Inc.
www.montyroberts.com
(888) U2 Monty

Flags

Flags Unlimited, Inc.
www.usflags.com
(800) 989-3524

Flag Holders

Gleason Mounted Supply Co.
www.gleasonmountedsupply.com
(800) 618-8735

Flares

Galls®
www.galls.com
(800) 477-7766

Horseshoes with Polyurethane Inserts

Slypner Athletic Horseshoes
www.slypner.com
(800) 759-7637

Mounted Police Supply

Gleason Mounted Supply Co.
www.gleasonmountedsupply.com
(800) 618-8735

Pelicano Equine Training

www.rickpelicano.com

Reflectors

Gleason Mounted Supply Co.
www.gleasonmountedsupply.com
(800) 618-8735

Valley Vet Supply Co.
www.valleyvet.com
(800) 419-9524

Stagecoach West
www.stagecoachwest.com
(800) 648-1121

Country Supply Co.
www.countrysupply.com
(800) 637-6721

Smoke Grenades

Force-Ten
www.force-ten.com
(360) 293-3793

E. Vernon Hill Inc.
www.evhill.com
(707) 584-9384

Smoke Machines

Novelty Lights Inc.
www.noveltylights.com
(800) 209-6122

World of Magic
www.best-price-fog-machines.com
(866) 966-9566

PHOTO AND ILLUSTRATION CREDITS

Anne Boccia
Pages 26, 79, 82, 99, 108-9, 129, 134, 146-7, 150, 167 (9.7 A&B)

Linda Emminizer
Pages 73, 125-6, 133, 136, 139

Janet Hitchen
Pages 27-8 (2.3 A&B), 53-59, 63-4, 72, 81, 85-87, 106, 110, 113, 116-7, 119-124, 130-132, 137

Mike McNally
Pages 114, 138

Dominic Pelicano
Pages 152-3, 167 (9.8)

Rick Pelicano
Pages 28 (2.3 C), 127, 151

Cartoon art by Gary Jones

Diagrams by Anne Boccia, except page 165, by Rick Pelicano

INDEX

The author as he appears in the documentary **Tournament.**